FAT CAT, FINICKY CAT

A Pet Owner's Guide to
Cat Food and Feline Nutrition

Karen Leigh Davis

With 76 photographs
Illustrations by Tana Hakanson

BARRON'S

Important Note

Always use caution and common sense whenever handling a cat, especially one that may be ill or injured. Employ proper restraint devices as necessary. In addition, if the information and procedures contained in this book differ in any way from your veterinarian's recommendations concerning your pet's health care, please consult him/her prior to their implementation. Finally, because each individual pet is unique, always consult your veterinarian before administering any type of treatment or medication to your pet.

All inquiries should be addressed to:
Barron's Educational Series, Inc.
250 Wireless Boulevard
Hauppauge, New York 11788

International Standard Book No. 0-8120-9853-6

Library of Congress Catalog Card No. 97-22431

Library of Congress Cataloging-in-Publication Data

Davis, Karen Leigh, 1953-
   Fat cat, finicky cat : a pet owner's guide to cat food and feline nutrition / Karen Leigh Davis.
        p.   cm.
   Includes bibliographical references (p. 148) and index.
   ISBN 0-8120-9853-6
   1. Cats—Food. 2. Cats—Nutrition. 3. Consumer
   education.
   I. Title.
SF447.6.D38   1997
636.8'085—dc21   97-22431
                                                   CIP

Printed in Hong Kong

987654321

About the Author

Karen Leigh Davis, a professional member of the Cat Writers' Association, has a background in journalism and business writing. She has written a pet care column and numerous feature articles on cats and other companion animals for national and regional magazines and newspapers. As s freelance writer with more than 15 years of experience, she has conducted extensive research on animal-related topics with veterinarians, breeders, and other experts. Davis comes from a cat-loving family and has a lifetime of experience living in the company of cats. She has bred and shown Persians and Himalayans, but she finds all felines, purebred or mixed, domestic or wild, irresistibly charming and beautiful. She lives in Roanoke, Virginia, with four Persian cats.

Other Barron's titles by Karen Leigh Davis:
Somali Cats (1996)
The Exotic Shorthair Cat (1997)

Photo Credits

Bob Schwartz: back cover, inside front cover, inside back cover, pages 9, 11, 13, 14, 15, 18, 19, 21, 22, 26, 35, 38, 40, 43, 46, 47, 48, 49, 53, 55, 60, 63, 66, 68, 69, 70, 72, 81, 85, 86, 87, 89, 90, 92, 97, 109, 110 top, 110 bottom, 111, 120, 121, 124, 126, 127, 129, 130, 138, 140; Bonnie Nance: pages 28, 29, 57, 61, 65, 116, 119; Paul Brown Imaging: pages 3, 4 top, 4 bottom, 5, 6, 8; Judith Strom: pages 23, 64, 77, 95; Joan Balzarini: pages 37, 79, 104, 132; Gulliver Spring: page 78; Jean Wentworth: page 32; Chanan: page 51; Derek Whitehouse Photography: page 2; Behling and Johnson: front cover (fat cat); Jean-Michel Labat: front cover (finicky cat).

Contents

Preface

This book is intended to be used as a pet owner's general reference and consumer guide to understanding cat foods and cat nutrition. It is not intended to replace the advice of a qualified veterinarian or good veterinary care. While every effort has been made to present current scientific opinions and to help ensure that no misleading information appears in this book, it is important to note that conflicting or inconclusive research exists on certain related topics. It is also important to note that ongoing research may bring to light important new discoveries at any time. Thus, use this book as an educational tool, to gain a basic knowledge and understanding of cat foods and nutrition so that you can make informed choices and protect your cats' general health and well-being.

Within these pages, you will learn how cat foods are made, how to read and decipher cat food labels, and how to select appropriate foods from the many choices on the market. If you have questions or experience difficulties while trying to find the right food for your cat, please contact a veterinarian. And always consult a veterinarian before putting your cat on any special diet. Remember, too, that no *one* perfect pet food exists for every cat. Every cat has its own individual nutritional needs, and what's more, those needs can change as the cat grows and matures.

Acknowledgments

I wish to thank David Dzanis, D.V.M., Ph.D., D.A.C.V.N., Veterinary Medical Officer and Pet Food Specialist for the Food and Drug Administration's Center for Veterinary Medicine, for evaluating this manuscript and for patiently answering my numerous questions; the Ralston Purina Company and the Waltham Centre for Pet Nutrition for inviting me to attend symposia and lectures on pet nutrition, for enabling me to tour their research facilities, for sharing research materials and nutrition information, and for allowing me to interview and consult their experts during the writing of this book; the Association of American Feed Control Officials, Inc., for providing information and for granting permission to reprint the nutrient profiles for cat foods; and, as always, Mary Falcon, Barron's Project Editor, for her patient guidance and skillful editing.

Chapter 1
Cat Food: A Brief History and Introduction

The Domesticated Cat

Food lies at the heart of humankind's long relationship with the domestic cat. Because large human communities tend to attract rodents that scavenge through feed stockpiles, feral felines probably first prowled into agricultural settlements looking for food, lured by the abundance of easy prey. History credits the ancient Egyptians with being among the first people to domesticate the cat about 3,500 years ago. The Egyptians were quick to realize the cat's immense value in protecting grain stores and harvests from rats and mice and, no doubt, began offering food to keep them around. As a result, the cat embarked on a long period of elevated status during this early era of civilization.

Archaeological discoveries tell us that the ancient Egyptians felt blessed to be in the company of cats. They worshiped cats as household gods, mourned the loss when one died, and mummified the remains for entry into the afterlife. In fact, so highly prized were these early domesticated felines by Egyptian society that killing one brought a sentence of death.

In time, domestication became a trade-off. In exchange for their natural pest control services, wild cats gradually adapted to an easier lifestyle as they spent more time sharing the human hearth. Increasingly, they depended on people for their survival. Today, this mutually beneficial relationship has evolved to a higher level of companionship but remains deeply rooted in the exchange of service for food.

From Field Mice to Gourmet Feasts

While most modern house cats no longer find it necessary to serve primarily as mousers, they continue to enrich our lives in countless other ways. As payback for the

Despite their independent natures, domestic cats rely on their owners to protect their well-being and provide complete and balanced nutrition.

pleasure and unconditional love cats give us, we humans return our affection in the form of special toys and treats. And because cats give us a lifetime of love and devoted companionship, many people feel their cats deserve the best food money can buy in exchange. Nowhere is this more eloquently expressed than in the array of gourmet cat food entrees lining grocery store shelves.

In spite of their reputation for being aloof, mysterious, haughty, frisky, and finicky, cats have become the most popular pets in America, easily outnumbering the family dog by several million. Acknowledging this trend, pet food companies spend millions researching, developing, marketing, and advertising cat food products designed to entice not only felines with discriminating tastes, but also the owners determined to please them.

For many decades, however, not much was known about cats' nutritional needs. Owners assumed that

their outdoor cats could simply fend for themselves and thrive on almost anything, from leftovers to live prey. Commercial pet food manufacturing did not become a thriving industry until after World War II, when the development of prepackaged foods and other modern conveniences became something of a national obsession. Before that, foods manufactured and marketed exclusively for cats were rare. More common, particularly in the early 1900s, were pet foods made from slaughterhouse cast-offs and labeled as suitable for both dogs and cats. Today, we know that the nutritional needs of dogs and cats are vastly different, and no single commercial formula exists that can adequately serve the needs of both species. Instead, dog food is for dogs, and cat foods are scientifically formulated for various feline life stages.

Armed with new scientific knowledge and spurred by consumer demand, the post-war pet food industry blossomed into a megabucks business, topping out at several billions of dollars annually in sales in recent years. Today, pet foods are among the most highly visible products in the media and on grocery store shelves, taking up as much space in the supermarket as breakfast cereals and soft drinks. Many manufacturers don't even sell through grocery stores; they position their products through distributors, pet shops, and pet supply warehouses. In addition, some product lines developed for the dietary management of specific medical conditions are available through veterinary clinics.

Pet Nutrition Research

All of the major pet food manufacturers maintain kennels and catteries with hundreds of dogs and cats that they use in daily feeding trials and other research programs to substantiate their product claims. The Paul F. Iams Technical Center is the research and development center for The Iams Company, founded in 1946 and maker of Iams and Eukanuba foods. The well-known Ralston Purina Company started animal nutrition studies at its Purina Pet Care Center in 1926. This 337-acre facility near St. Louis, Missouri, houses as many as 900 dogs and 700 cats at any one time. Studies conducted there have helped experts determine pets' taste preferences and better understand the relationship diet has to hair coat, reproduction, and hip dysplasia. Similarly, the Waltham Centre for Pet Nutrition (WCPN) in Leicestershire, England, has made significant contributions to the collective pool of knowledge on companion animal nutrition, health, behavior, and husbandry. For example, research carried out at WCPN confirmed the need for a dietary source of the vital nutrient, taurine, and helped determine the level necessary to maintain adult cats' optimum health. WCPN also helped establish guidelines for determining pets' energy requirements and identified differences in the way dogs and cats eat and digest their food. Many manufacturers' research programs have supported animal nutrition studies at major universities or otherwise contributed significantly to our overall knowledge of feline nutrition.

There is little doubt that our modern-day cats have benefited from this ongoing pet food research. The pet-owning public also has benefited by having more accurate and abundant nutrition information available than ever before. And with an ever-increasing awareness and interest in all types of fitness and nutrition matters, more and more owners are educating themselves about nutrition facts so they can

During feeding trials, staff members at the Waltham Centre for Pet Nutrition weigh each cat and chart how well it maintains its condition on a particular food.

Feeding trial portions are carefully weighed, measured, and controlled. Ultimately, this helps the pet food manufacturer determine the amount an average cat needs to eat to stay healthy.

help their cats live longer, healthier lives, free from illnesses caused by dietary deficiencies or excesses. Recognizing this trend, reputable pet food manufacturers keep striving to develop or improve products that consumers want and cats like.

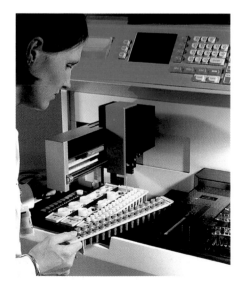

Using high-tech methods, researchers carefully analyze and record blood values and other clinical observations during feeding trials.

The National Research Council (NRC)

Scientific research in pet nutrition also has benefited animals and their owners by setting minimum standards for the nutritional content of cat foods that have been adopted industry-wide. The Subcommittee on Cat Nutrition of the National Academy of Science's National Research Council (NRC) established minimum nutritional requirements for cats in its scientific publication titled *Nutrient Requirements of Cats*. The report provides guidelines for applying the known nutrient requirements to feline diets in at least the minimal amounts to sustain health, growth, and reproduction. These recommendations are widely used by cat food manufacturers for formulating foods. In cases where concrete data on certain obscure nutrients remains unavailable, the publication offers only estimates, based on amounts known to give satisfactory performance in other species. Last revised in 1986, the NRC publication is due to be updated by a panel of animal nutritionists and other experts.

The AAFCO Protocols

The Association of American Feed Control Officials (AAFCO) has also established cat food nutrient profiles, using the NRC requirements as a basis, but interpreting and applying the data in terms of the practical considerations inherent in formulating feed. In addition to nutrient profiles, AAFCO also has established testing protocols that are widely used in the industry for substantiating the nutritional claims of pet foods through animal feeding trials. A decade ago, it was common to read a cat food label that said, "guaranteed to meet or exceed all NRC requirements" for feline nutrition. Today, however, the major pet food manufacturers use AAFCO's nutrient profiles and testing protocols to formulate and substantiate the nutrient content of their products. Instead of references to the NRC, labels on store shelves today say something similar to: "[Product name] is formulated to meet the nutritional levels established by AAFCO Cat Food Nutrient Profiles for all life stages."

Each product tested according to AAFCO protocols is fed to cats and kittens under controlled conditions for a specified period of time. A veterinarian evaluates the animals periodically, and researchers carefully record all clinical observations, including body weight, blood values, and reproductive ability. If no animals die, lose condition, or show signs of nutritional deficiency or excess during the feeding trial, the product passes the test. Once substantiated in this manner, a product can rightfully carry the endorsement, "Animal feeding tests using AAFCO procedures substantiate that [product name] provides complete and balanced nutrition for all life stages of cats." For different life-cycle formulas the words "all life stages" may be substituted with a specific life stage—such as growth (for kittens), gestation and lactation

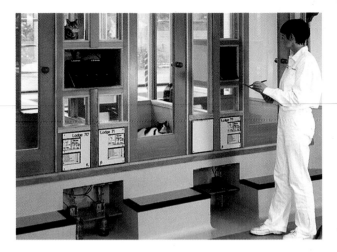

(for pregnant and nursing queens), or adult maintenance (for full-grown cats)—providing the product has passed the specific testing procedures established for the particular life stage named. Life-cycle nutrition is discussed in more detail later—see p. 65.

How the Industry Is Regulated

Established in 1909, AAFCO consists of officials from Canada and the United States who develop and propose regulations related to the production and labeling of animal feeds. To accomplish this, AAFCO officials work closely with the Food and Drug Administration's Center for Veterinary Medicine (FDA-CVM), which helps set standards for the content and quality of animal foods. The regulations are aimed at protecting consumers from deceptive claims as well as safeguarding the health of animals. They are published annually in AAFCO's book,

Urine is collected through a special system and routinely analyzed to determine the impact of certain foods on feline urinary tract health.

Research cats at the Waltham Centre for Pet Nutrition live indoors in clean, spacious quarters designed especially for their health and comfort. Although many of the cats are involved in life-long projects, others are placed in homes when they are no longer needed.

company selling a cat food that does not meet a particular state's regulations can be warned, can have the product seized, and can even be prohibited from marketing that product in that state until the violation is corrected.

AAFCO's model pet food regulations, as outlined in the *Official Publication,* are designed primarily to help ensure that pet food labels are not misleading and that consumers receive accurate nutritional information about the pet foods they buy. Pet food products are also subject to some of the same laws that govern human foods, in addition to those that regulate animal feed. For example, the Federal Food, Drug and Cosmetic Act regulates food distribution in interstate commerce and prohibits the shipment of adulterated or misbranded pet foods. A food is considered to be *adulterated* if it contains contaminants or potentially harmful substances. A *misbranded* food is one that bears a false, misleading, or incomplete label. Any product that is adulterated or misbranded is in violation of the act and subject to penalty.

State feed control offices have the responsibility of enforcing state laws that govern the sale, inspection, and labeling of livestock feed and pet foods. Most of these laws are patterned after a list of regulations called the Model Bill, developed cooperatively by industry leaders and AAFCO officials.

The U.S. Department of Agriculture (USDA) is charged with ensuring

which is simply titled *Official Publication.* The AAFCO guidelines are endorsed by the American Feed Industry Association and the Pet Food Institute, both of which are industry organizations that provide advice on animal food regulations.

Even though AAFCO helps set the rules for the industry, it functions primarily as an advisory body, not a government agency, and therefore has no authority to enforce the rules. Enforcement must be done at the state level. In the United States, each state can choose to model its own feed control laws after AAFCO's official pet food regulations. Fortunately, most state governments have chosen to adopt AAFCO's regulations into state law, so that pet food manufacturers adhering to them benefit by being able to market labels that satisfy requirements from state to state, nationwide. This also encourages a considerable degree of uniformity in the industry, because a

that slaughtered animal carcasses or parts intended for pet food are handled and shipped in such a way as to not be mistaken for human food. This usually involves marking the product with charcoal or dye. The USDA also sees that pet food packages are clearly labeled so as not to be mistaken for human food.

While the FDA and AAFCO work closely together to ensure that pet food labels are not misleading, the Federal Trade Commission regulates pet food advertising to help prevent false or misleading statements from appearing in television commercials or other media.

"Complete and Balanced" Claims

If a cat food claims to be nutritionally "complete," it must contain a formula of nutrients—amino acids, proteins, carbohydrates, fats, minerals, and vitamins—essential for maintaining life when fed as the sole, daily ration. These nutrients are necessary in varying amounts at different stages of a cat's life to support growth, reproduction, and adult maintenance. Therefore, if a cat food is "balanced," it contains all of the known required nutrients in proper amounts and proportions recommended for either a particular life stage, as stated on the label, or for all life stages.

According to regulations, manufacturers can state on their labels that their products provide "complete and balanced" nutrition *only* if this claim has been substantiated

ANIMAL FEEDING TESTS USING AAFCO PROCEDURES SUBSTANTIATE THAT THIS CAT FOOD PROVIDES COMPLETE AND BALANCED NUTRITION FOR THE MAINTENANCE OF ADULT CATS

either by adhering to a proven formulation or by animal feeding trials. Although more expensive and time-consuming, substantiation by feeding trials on live animals is considered the most reliable method because the actual effects of the food can be observed over a period of time.

A cat food label also will tell you whether the product is designed to meet the nutritional needs of kittens, adult cats, pregnant and nursing cats, or cats of all life stages. So, when selecting a food for your cat's daily ration, look for this information on the package and choose only the ones labeled as complete and balanced for your cat's current life stage. If a pet food product doesn't state on the label that it is complete and balanced, you can safely assume that it isn't designed to be fed as a daily ration. (See page 58.) Snack foods and treats, for example, usually aren't labeled as complete and balanced (although some are) because they are exempt from this

Manufacturers substantiate claims that their cat food offers complete and balanced nutrition in one of two ways: by adhering to a proven formula or by testing the food in animal feeding trials. The method used is disclosed in the product's statement of nutritional adequacy.

In exchange for feeding and taking care of them, cats give us the pleasure of their companionship and unconditional love.

labeling requirement. They are exempt because they are clearly declared as a "snack" or "treat for cats" and are thus intended to be fed intermittently or on a complementary basis, and not as a substitute for daily meals. While they are OK for occasional use, treats and snacks should never replace whole rations of a regular cat food that is labeled as complete and balanced.

It is generally understood that snacks are snacks, but some foods intended for temporary or supplemental use may be easily confused with complete, daily rations. For example, some therapeutic foods are intended for limited use in the management of certain medical conditions. Such foods are not exempt and must be labeled "for intermittent or supplemental feeding only," or with words that convey a similar meaning. Determining how the product is intended to be fed is just one more good reason why it's important to always read the label before purchasing a cat food.

Chapter 2
The ABCs of Feline Nutrition

The Carnivorous Cat

The basis of any good cat food is meat, or animal protein. In fact, the scientific community often refers to cats as *obligate* carnivores, meaning that they must eat meat to stay healthy. This does not mean, however, that an *all*-meat or *all*-fish diet is healthier for them than a diet that simply contains sufficient meat. Quite the opposite is true. Cats also require important nutrients that come from plant sources. Under natural conditions, feral cats generally consume most or all of the body parts of their small mammal prey, including any plant material that happens to remain in the stomach. This material provides important nutrients, such as fiber, calcium, and B vitamins, generally not found in adequate amounts in an all-meat diet. While ground, grilled, or chopped mouse in a can may be the most "natural" cat food, the chances of such a product going over well with the human consumer who has to buy it are nil. Because pet food manufacturers must satisfy *two* consumers—the cat and the owner—historically they have used culturally accepted foodstuffs as protein sources—fish, poultry, beef—and added cereals, grains, and synthetic vitamins and minerals, as necessary, to achieve the recommended nutrient balance established by scientific research.

Being a natural carnivore, the cat must have enough animal protein in its diet to stay healthy. In the wild, small mammals and birds would supply the necessary nutrients.

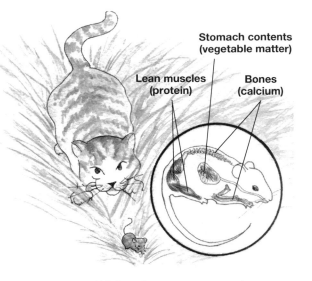

Stomach contents
(vegetable matter)

Lean muscles
(protein)

Bones
(calcium)

A Is for Amino Acids

Amino acids—more than 20 of them—are important chemical components cats need to synthesize body proteins. Many experts describe them as the building blocks of protein because protein (see also the section "P Is for Protein") is made up of amino acids, and without them the feline body cannot effectively use the food it consumes. Amino acids are divided into two groups: essential and nonessential. The cat's body can manufacture nonessential amino acids in sufficient amounts to maintain good health. But essential amino acids must come from the diet because cats cannot manufacture them on their own. Essential amino acids required by cats include:

An all-meat diet is not complete and balanced for cats. In the wild, they consume plant material containing valuable fiber and nutrients from the stomachs of their live prey.

While plant source nutrients are beneficial, it is important to note that cats cannot thrive on a vegetarian diet. Although humans may elect to be vegetarians for noble health or moral reasons, nature intended for cats to be predatory carnivores. Having evolved as such, cats require much more protein than either humans or dogs, and while *some* of that protein can come from plant sources, a certain amount *must* come from animal sources. Cats simply cannot remain healthy for long on foods made solely from plant sources. To be nutritionally complete and balanced, a cat food designed to be fed to a feline every day as its staple diet must contain the proper amounts of plant and animal protein, plus the right mixture of amino acids, carbohydrates, fats, minerals, and vitamins. These nutrients are discussed as follows.

Arginine
Histidine
Isoleucine
Leucine
Lysine
Methionine
Phenylalanine
Taurine
Threonine
Tryptophan
Valine

One or more of these essential amino acids may be listed as an additive on a cat food label. Those not listed on the label occur naturally in the cat food ingredients. Without sufficient amounts of these essential amino acids in the diet, cats cannot remain healthy. Kittens can experience stunted growth if their diets lack essential amino acids. Symptoms of an amino acid or protein deficiency may include weight loss, appetite loss, overall poor condition, muscle spasms, drooling, cataracts, and incoordination.

Arginine helps convert ammonia, a toxic byproduct of protein metabolism, into urea so that it can be safely excreted from the body in the urine. Because cats cannot manufacture sufficient amounts of arginine in their livers, they must obtain this essential amino acid from their diets. Otherwise, a deficiency could cause a dangerous buildup of ammonia in the blood. Fortunately, this condition rarely occurs in cats fed complete and balanced commercial diets. However, cats may be put at risk of a deficiency when allowed to subsist solely on "people food" and table scraps or when exclusively fed a homemade diet that has not been recommended or supervised by a veterinarian.

Taurine is an especially important nutrient for felines. While not considered to be a true amino acid because it is not a part of protein, taurine has long been listed with other amino acids and is still commonly discussed with them. However, AAFCO's 1997 Cat Food Nutrient Profiles removed taurine from the "Protein" nutrient list, which names the amino acids, and placed it under the heading with

"Vitamins & Others" (see page 142). It's not a vitamin either, but rather is one of the "other" nutrients.

Regardless of what you call it, taurine is an *essential* nutrient because, according to the experts, cats are the only known mammals that cannot manufacture enough taurine on their own for good health. Sufficient amounts must be supplied in the feline diet, whether it occurs naturally in the animal protein content or is added as a supplement. Taurine deficiency can cause *dilated cardiomyopathy*, which is a heart disease, and *central retinal degeneration*, which is an eye problem that can lead to blindness. Years ago, when taurine deficiency was first linked to these heart and eye problems in cats, responsible pet food manufacturers began adding more of this essential nutrient to their products. Today, high-quality, complete and balanced cat foods contain enough taurine to help ensure good health. Canned cat foods typically have more taurine added to

Kittens need more protein than adult cats to support the extra demands on their growing bodies. Without proper amounts of amino acids and other essential nutrients, they may experience stunted growth.

their formulas than do dry foods, because the canning process appears to affect taurine availability. Because of their special need for taurine, cats should never be fed a steady diet of dog food. Dog chow simply does not contain enough taurine (or protein) to promote good health in cats.

C Is for Carbohydrates

Carbohydrates are starches, sugars, cereals, and grain fibers. Common sources in cat foods are processed rice, soy, corn, wheat, barley, oats, and corn gluten meal. Carbohydrates are used in commercial cat feeds as important sources of energy and fiber. They break down into glucose, a simple sugar that provides energy to the body's cells. Although carbohydrate requirements

have not been established for cats, the NRC publication, the *Nutrient Requirements of Cats,* reports that the average dry commercial cat foods contain about 40 percent carbohydrate, most of which comes from cereals and grains. The grinding, flaking, and cooking methods used to process these cereal grains tend to improve the food's taste and digestibility, according to industry experts.

E Is for Energy

Although not a nutrient, the need for energy to carry out the body's normal functions is the reason why we and all other animals eat. The carbohydrates, proteins, and fats in foods provide our energy requirements. Energy is measured in *calories.* Technically speaking, a calorie is the amount of heat needed to raise the temperature of water by 1 degree Celsius. Because this amount is so small, the energy content of food is commonly expressed in *kilocalories.* One kilocalorie (kcal) actually equals 1,000 *small* calories, which are units used primarily for scientific measurements in physics and chemistry. But the amount of energy in 1 kcal also is often expressed as a *big* calorie, which is the unit used in human nutrition and generally designated by a capital *C.* This is why, when referring to food and nutrition topics, you will often hear the terms *kilocalorie* and *calorie* used interchangeably.

Far from being just "fillers" in cat food, cereals, grains, and other starches provide energy, fiber, B-complex vitamins, and other nutrients.

Energy is measured three ways: Gross Energy (GE), Digestible Energy (DE), and Metabolizable Energy (ME). Gross energy is the total energy content of a food. Because no animal is capable of extracting the total or gross energy from food, we must also measure how much energy an animal can actually absorb or digest (DE) and how much energy an animal actually uses or metabolizes (ME).

The gross energy of a food is first established by burning it in a special chamber and measuring it with an instrument called a calorimeter. Then, animal feeding trials can determine the amounts of digestible and metabolizable energy. The GE eaten minus the GE lost in the feces equals the digestible energy. Metabolizable energy accounts for what is also lost in the urine. Although not required, the energy content of cat food, when given on the package label, is stated in ME, and AAFCO has established specific protocols for measuring and substantiating the ME in pet foods. Calorie content, when given, must be ME expressed in kilocalories per kilogram or "kcal/kg."

Because the energy requirements of kittens and pregnant or nursing queens is much higher, these animals generally require food with more digestible protein, fats, and carbohydrates than non-breeding adults. According to NRC estimates, an adult cat requires about 32 kcal of ME per pound of

Carbohydrates, fats, and proteins in the diet provide energy for normal metabolism and playful, kittenish antics.

body weight. This means an average 7-pound cat would require about 224 kcals per day. It's important to remember, however, that the proper amount to feed depends on the caloric needs of the individual animal and on the type and quality of food given.

F Is for Fiber

The fiber content of complex carbohydrates provides bulk, also called roughage, which helps regulate the movement of food through the cat's intestines. Fiber content in pet food is reported on the label as "crude fiber," which is a rough estimate at best. Common fiber sources in pet foods include guar gum, wheat bran, corn, and beans. The various chemical components of fiber are often referred to as cellulose, lignin, pectins, gums, or mucilages.

The effects of dietary fiber vary with the type of fiber present and with the way it's processed. Different types of fiber take up more or less water in the intestinal tract, thereby changing the speed at which food passes through the gut. This particular property makes fiber an important tool in the treatment of constipation or chronic diarrhea.

The amount of fiber fed is also important. Too much fiber in the diet can cause excessive gas, loose stools, or increased stool volume. The often-stated rule of thumb is all too true: "More fiber in, more feces out." In fact, foods containing too much poor-quality fiber can actually have a negative impact on feline health by slowing the absorption

and hampering the digestibility of vital nutrients.

Specially designed, good-quality, high-fiber foods can be beneficial in the treatment of certain disorders, such as obesity, diabetes, and bowel disease. Because they are often used to manage medical conditions, these special diets are generally sold through veterinarians. Fiber is also thought to provide some protection against certain cancer-causing toxins by binding with them and preventing their absorption into the bloodstream.

F Is Also for Fats

Dietary fats, also called *lipids*, provide more calories and concentrated energy than carbohydrates or proteins. They are either saturated or unsaturated. Saturated fats are solid at room temperature, while unsaturated fats are liquid. Two fatty acids are essential to cats: linoleic acid and arachidonic acid. Linoleic acid is available in vegetable oils, whereas arachidonic acid is available to cats only from animal fat. Other animals can convert linoleic acid to arachidonic acid, but cats cannot. They must derive the latter substance from animal sources, which is another reason why cats must have meat in their diets.

Just as a higher fat content can make food taste better to humans, the same is true for cats. In fact, manufacturers may add more fat

Excellent nutrition is essential for keeping this beautiful Persian's show coat in top form.

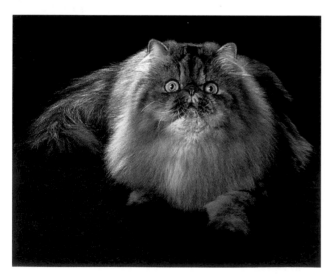

14

and protein to some foods just to enhance the taste, or palatability. As expected, such foods are also usually higher in calories, since fats contain more than twice the calories of protein or carbohydrates. Of course, cats cannot tell how many fats and calories are in their food. They simply eat what tastes good to them, and they eat until they feel full and satisfied.

Unless a cat is overweight, health-conscious humans need not worry about their cats' fat consumption. For one thing, fats help make your cat's coat shiny and healthy looking. Also, feline fat requirements differ vastly from ours. Cats readily tolerate higher levels of fat in their daily diet than humans. In fact, cats seem to have evolved with a much more efficient way of metabolizing and handling cholesterol, a type of lipid well-known for the health complications it can cause in humans when present in too-high amounts. Prepared pet foods often contain a lot of beef tallow, which is rich in saturated fats, yet cats don't seem to develop atherosclerosis and related coronary artery disease the way people do. The reason for this may be because cats have a lot more of the good cholesterol than the bad. "Good" cholesterol, or high-density lipoproteins (HDL), carry cholesterol out of the body's tissues to the liver for disposal. "Bad" cholesterol, or low-density lipoproteins (LDL), carry cholesterol to the body tissues. In cats, the ratio of good to bad, or

HDL to LDL, is 4 to 1; in humans the ratio is reverse. Why cats are able to maintain higher levels of HDL than LDL is not yet well understood, but research supported by the Waltham Centre for Pet Nutrition in Leicestershire, England, is currently underway to learn more about cholesterol in cats.

Fats not only enhance the taste of cat food, they are important carriers of fat-soluble vitamins. Fat sources in the feline diet may include fish oil, soybean oil, wheat germ oil, and animal fat. As mentioned previously, fats also help maintain a healthy skin and hair coat. Symptoms of essential fatty acid deficiency include a dull coat, flaking skin, hair loss, crusty sores, frequent illness, listlessness, and overall poor condition. Studies show that linoleic acid deficiency can impair growth and reproduction and affect the kidneys, connective tissues, and red blood cells.

Complete and balanced nutrition is essential for successful feline reproduction. Improper amounts of certain vitamins, minerals, and essential fatty acids can compromise the health of mother cats and kittens.

M Is for Minerals

Cats need certain minerals to help synthesize vitamins, produce hormones, promote normal bone growth, transport oxygen in the blood, maintain fluid and electrolyte balance, and aid in muscle and nerve functions. For good health, cats need proper amounts of calcium, phosphorus, sodium, chloride, iron, potassium, magnesium, iodine, copper, zinc, manganese, and selenium. To a lesser extent, it is believed that cats also require, as do some other animals, the trace minerals sulfur, fluorine, chromium, tin, silicon, nickel, molybdenum, and vanadium. However, because of a lack of published data, the NRC's "Nutrient Requirements of Cats" contains no recommended requirements for these trace elements.

Some minerals occur naturally in the ingredients that make up cat food and, therefore, may not appear on the cat food label. Minerals added to supplement the ingredient mix may be listed on a label as bone meal (phosphorus, calcium), sodium (salt), cobalt carbonate, phosphoric acid, manganese sulfate, potassium iodide, zinc sulfate, and ferrous sulfate (iron), among others.

Because many minerals must work together in proper proportions to perform interrelated functions, too much of one can be just as harmful as too little. For this reason, dietary supplements, unless recommended by a veterinarian, are not necessary and should be avoided when feeding a high-quality, complete and balanced commercial cat food.

Magnesium is just one of several dietary constituents blamed in the past as a contributing factor in feline urologic syndrome (FUS). FUS is a potentially life-threatening disease caused by tiny mineral crystals that form in the urinary tract, leading to painful irritation and sometimes serious blockages. Today, most veterinarians refer to this condition as FLUTD or LUTD, which stands for feline lower urinary tract disease, an umbrella term for related disorders. Warning signs include visiting the litter box frequently, urinating in unusual places, straining to urinate, and passing blood-tinged urine.

Studies clearly implicate a connection between FUS and high magnesium levels in the feline diet, leading many laymen to believe that this essential nutrient is bad. However, current findings indicate that the overall mineral composition of cat food, rather than an excess of any single ingredient, plays a greater role in maintaining the body's acid-base balance than was previously understood. The acid-base conditions determine whether the urine pH stays within normal acidic ranges or becomes too alkaline. The higher (more alkaline) the urine pH, the more favorable are conditions for mineral crystals to form in the urinary tract. Carnivores typically produce an acid urine,

Minerals: What They're Important For

Calcium (Ca)	Strong bones and teeth, normal blood clotting, nerve transmission
Phosphorus (P)	Normal bone development
Sodium (Na)	Normal meabolism, fluid regulation, transfer of nutrients to cells
Chloride (Cl)	Normal metabolism, formation of hydrochloric acid in the stomach
Potassium (K)	Maintains fluid balance and proper nerve, enzyme, immune system functions
Magnesium (Mg)	Component of muscle and bone, influences enzymatic reactions
Iron (Fe)	Helps form hemoglobin, the oxygen-carrying component of red blood cells
Zinc (Zn)	Activates important enzymes and aids normal protein metabolism
Copper (Cu)	Helps prevent anemia, important for iron metabolism and connective tissue
Manganese (Mn)	Important for reproduction and proper bone formation, activates enzymes
Selenium (Se)	Works with vitaminn E to act as an antioxidant in the body
Cobalt (Co)	Component of vitamin B12, which is critical to certain metabolism functions
Iodine (I)	Production of thyroid hormones by the thyroid gland

whereas, plant-eating animals tend to produce an alkaline urine. The cat has evolved to produce a normal urine pH of 6.0 to 7.0, according to the NRC. Above 7.0, crystals are more likely to occur, while at the lower levels, the acid urine helps dissolve waste crystals or prevent them from forming in the first place.

Without attention to the overall mineral composition, cat foods with a high vegetable or cereal content can cause the cat to produce an alkaline urine. For this reason, allowing cats to nibble free-choice on dry foods throughout the day was once discouraged, because it was thought that this practice predisposed cats to FUS. This opinion

Changes in litter box behavior may indicate kidney problems or feline lower urinary tract disease (FLUTD), a disorder that has been linked with diet.

ter basis. For growth and reproduction formulas, AAFCO's minimum recommended amount is 0.08 percent. Magnesium levels should not exceed 0.12 percent.

Ash, another dietary constituent previously incriminated in FUS, is a term of bygone days that has no connection to urinary-tract health, as was once believed. Ash actually refers to the residue left after a food's mineral content has been burned at a high temperature. A food claiming to have "low ash" content meant that very little of this residue was left after burning. Consumers tended to misinterpret these claims to mean "low magnesium," which was not necessarily the case, since magnesium is only one mineral component of ash. Nowadays, however, "low ash" claims should no longer be seen on cat food labels.

Calcium and phosphorus are important for strong bones and teeth, normal blood clotting, and proper nerve transmission. A deficiency during a kitten's first year can produce soft, deformed bones. In adults, a deficiency can contribute to a bone-thinning condition called *hyperparathyroidism*. This condition develops when the parathyroid glands detect too-low levels of calcium in the blood. The glands respond by releasing a hormone that extracts stored calcium from the bones to counteract the imbalance. If the imbalance remains uncorrected, this continued parathyroid response thins the bones over a

began to change, however, after responsible pet food manufacturers, armed with the latest scientific knowledge, started adding acidifying ingredients to their formulas to help keep urine pH within safely acidic ranges. Today, most commercial cat foods, including dry foods, are believed to contain enough acidifying ingredients to help maintain normal pH balance.

While urinary acidity is the most important factor in lower urinary tract disease, magnesium content in cat food remains a secondary concern, enough to warrant restricting dietary levels when managing recurrent bouts of FUS. It's important to remember, however, that, while excesses should be avoided, the feline body requires magnesium for bone growth and metabolic functions. The NRC recommends a minimum of 400 milligrams per kilogram (mg/kg) per day, or 0.04 percent, on a dry mat-

period of time, making them brittle and prone to fracture easily. To avoid irreversible skeletal abnormalities, kittens need, for their first full year, a high-quality, commercial cat food designed specifically to support feline growth. Also, avoid homemade diets comprised solely of meat, as these are not complete and balanced and can contribute to a calcium deficiency as well.

Because calcium and phosphorus must interact to maintain certain body functions, the two minerals need to be present in the diet at recommended ratios ranging from 1:1 or 1.5:1 to 2:1 (that is, 1 or 1 and ½ to 2 parts calcium to each 1 part phosphorus). Feeding a calcium or mineral supplement along with a complete and balanced cat food can alter this delicate ratio and be just as detrimental to normal bone development as a deficit. Excessive amounts of either mineral also can inhibit the body's absorption of magnesium and other minerals.

Sodium and chloride, supplied as salt, are essential for the body's metabolism and fluid balance. In addition, chloride aids in protein digestion by forming the stomach enzyme hydrochloric acid. Deficiencies of these two minerals in cats are rare but are characterized by weight loss, hair loss, and dry skin. However, cats suffering severe or repeated bouts of vomiting and diarrhea have an increased risk of deficiency and fluid imbalance. While lightly salting a cat's food is sometimes recommended to make

it drink more water, this practice is generally unnecessary and perhaps even unsafe without the advice of a veterinarian. What's more, making the food taste *too* salty may actually make the cat refuse the food altogether.

Potassium is especially important for electrolyte balance and for proper nerve, muscle, and immune system functions. Potassium depletion can occur in conjunction with fluid loss due to severe vomiting, chronic diarrhea, or kidney disease. A significant potassium deficiency can interrupt normal heart muscle function with fatal consequences. Deficiency signs include weakness, dehydration, appetite loss, weight loss, poor growth (in kittens), locomotion problems, and unkempt fur.

Iron and copper, together with vitamin B12, help prevent anemia, a blood disorder characterized by reduced hemoglobin and red blood cell count. Hemoglobin is the red

Along with good breeding, the quality of nutrition these kittens receive in their first year may make the difference between a mediocre show cat and a grand champion.

blood cell pigment that carries the oxygen in the blood to the body's cells. Under natural conditions, red blood cells are constantly used up and replaced throughout life, and proper absorption of iron from the small intestine is vital to this replenishment process. Copper assists with this normal iron metabolism. It also helps in the formation of connective tissue among the body's various parts and contributes to the normal production of skin pigment.

Zinc can cause copper and iron deficiency if present in the diet in excessive amounts over too long a period of time. Fortunately, this situation rarely develops. Zinc apparently activates several important body enzymes that aid in the metabolism of certain nutrients and that protect cells from oxidation damage. Although uncommon in the cat, zinc deficiency can impair sperm production in the male cat. Other deficiency signs include skin

disorders, weight loss, poor growth (in kittens), and an overall decline in condition. Excess calcium in the diet can render zinc useless in the cat's body, preventing its absorption and impairing important metabolic functions. But this, too, is not likely to be a problem when feeding a complete and balanced cat food made from high-quality ingredients.

Manganese is a metallic element present in the body in trace amounts, but its importance should not be underestimated. Like zinc, manganese appears to be an important activator of certain enzymes needed for amino acid metabolism and other essential processes. Manganese is also necessary for normal reproduction and bone growth. Excessive amounts of calcium and phosphorus may hamper the absorption of manganese from the intestinal tract.

Iodine is necessary for healthy thyroid function. The thyroid gland produces hormones that regulate the rate of the body's basal metabolism. Iodine deficiency can result in *hypothyroidism,* an underactive thyroid, a serious disorder requiring medical treatment. Treatment typically consists of lifelong supplementation with synthetic thyroid hormone. Signs include extreme lethargy, dull coat, hair loss, scaly skin, and weight gain. Iodine may be added to cat food in the form of potassium iodide, potassium iodate, sodium iodide, and calcium iodate.

Selenium works with vitamin E to act as an antioxidant. Antioxidants, present in certain foods, function at the cellular level to protect the body against cell damage from too many "free radicals." Free radicals are unstable oxygen molecules, produced during normal body metabolism, that can steal electrons from stable molecules, triggering potentially detrimental chemical changes called *oxidation.* Antioxidants exist to keep these renegade free radicals in check, thereby minimizing cell damage. Although an important nutrient for its antioxidant properties with vitamin E, selenium is known to be toxic to many animals at higher than the trace levels normally found in the body.

P Is for Protein

Protein promotes growth and tissue repair and sustains the immune system in all mammals. Primary sources of protein include the lean muscle meats, while secondary sources include whole cereal grains and soybean meal. Cats need protein for energy. Unlike humans, cats cannot use carbohydrates or fats in place of protein to supply all of their calories and energy needs. (Refer also to the section "A Is for Amino Acids.")

According to AAFCO's nutrient profiles for cats, protein should form at least 26 percent of an adult maintenance diet and at least 30 percent of a growth and reproduction formula. Many foods contain more, some as much as 45 percent. On a cat food label, protein content is expressed as "crude protein," an estimate that guarantees the minimum amount, *but not the actual amount*, present in the food. The word *crude* simply means that the percentage was determined by laboratory trial.

Older cats, particular those with kidney problems, may do better on a lower-protein (but high-quality)

Once weaned, active kittens need to be fed a high-quality growth and reproduction cat food, or one formulated for "all life stages," to ensure that they receive enough protein and other essential nutrients.

Carnivores by nature, cats must consume enough animal protein to satisfy their need for taurine and other important nutrients. They cannot thrive on a vegetarian diet.

21

Fish is a common source of animal protein in commercial cat foods, but an all-fish diet can lead to certain deficiencies.

protein percentages on cat food labels can be easily misinterpreted unless you use a standard method of comparison, such as dry weight comparison (see page 60).

To the cat, animal protein sources, such as beef, lamb, chicken, fish meal, or turkey, are especially important because they contain most or all of the essential amino acids. But as important as protein and meat are to the cat, too much is likely to be just as harmful as too little. However, some owners mistakenly believe that more meat is better for their carnivorous pets and will lavish them with exclusive diets of liver, fish, and beef, when in fact an all-meat or all-fish diet can lead to certain deficiency symptoms and disorders (see pages 80 and 83). These deficiencies do not necessarily stem from an excess of protein, but rather from an improper balance of calcium and other important minerals and vitamins. Meat alone is simply not a balanced meal and cannot provide the cat with all of the required nutrients.

To avoid such deficiencies, choose only complete and balanced cat foods. These contain all the protein and other nutrients your cat needs. For variety, these foods come in a wide selection of protein sources, from different kinds of fish to poultry, to lamb and other meats, to meat byproducts. Meat byproducts are simply animal parts and cuts of meat not generally used for human consumption, such as the heart, brain, tongue, and stomach.

diet, while growing kittens and pregnant or nursing queens need much more protein to support the extra demands placed on their bodies. In general, cats need about one and one half to two times more protein than dogs, which is one reason why you should never feed a cat dog food exclusively.

Because cats cannot store excess protein, they must consume the required amount daily from their food. Cat foods usually contain protein from both plant and animal sources; however, the label doesn't state which source is present in greater amount. Although pet food ingredients are supposed to be listed on a label in descending order of predominance by weight, this can still be misleading. For example, meat may be listed first, leading the consumer to believe that the product contains mostly meat, when in fact the summation of separately listed grains and cereals makes plant material the predominant ingredient. In addition,

Dry foods often are sprayed with a protein "digest," which is a liquefied, chemically predigested meat added primarily to enhance palatability.

The protein quality and digestibility are even more important than the quantity. The term *digestibility* refers to the amount of the protein present in a food that can actually be absorbed and used by the animal that eats it. The amount that can't be used is excreted as waste. Protein digestibility can be established only through feeding trials. Two different products may list the same percentage of protein on their packages, but controlled feeding studies may reveal very different levels of digestibility. A higher percentage of digestibility means that more of the protein content in the food can be used for energy, while less is wasted. In general, higher-quality premium cat foods provide greater protein digestibility.

V Is for Vitamins

With few exceptions, most vitamins cannot be manufactured internally and must be obtained from the diet. As long as the cat owner feeds a complete and balanced cat food, vitamin supplements are rarely necessary and should not be given, unless recommended by a veterinarian. Overdoses of certain vitamins, such as A and D, can be toxic to cats. Limited research has been conducted on feline vitamin requirements; however, the NRC

provides recommended minimum daily allowances for vitamins A, B complex, D, and E. Cats can manufacture their own vitamins C and K. Felines have an especially high requirement for the B complex vitamins—thiamine, riboflavin, niacin, biotin, and so on—particularly during periods of stress, illness, growth, or lactation. Sensitive to heat, light, moisture, and rancidity, vitamins are easily destroyed if food isn't prepared, packaged, and stored properly. Vitamin sources in cat foods may be listed as brewer's yeast (B complex), menadione (vitamin K), choline, lecithin, and folic acid, among others.

Vitamins are classified as either fat-soluble or water-soluble. Fat-soluble vitamins require the presence of fat in the diet for proper absorption to take place, whereas water-soluble vitamins depend on adequate water for that purpose. Like many minerals, vitamins work together and with other nutrients to

Vitamin and mineral supplements generally are not necessary when you feed your cats a good quality, complete and balanced commercial cat food.

Fat-Soluble Vitamins: What They're Important For

A (retinol)	Healthy vision, cell membrane regulation, growth
D (ergocalciferol, cholecalciferol)	Calcium and phosphorus metabolism, bone growth
E (tocopherol)	Antioxidant properties, aids normal reproduction
K (menadione, synthetic form)	Aids in normal blood clotting

perform their necessary functions, which is why adding unwarranted supplements to the diet can upset this delicate balance and cause detrimental side effects.

Vitamin A: Cats require *preformed* vitamin A in their diets because they lack the ability to convert beta-carotene; the plant source of vitamin A, into the active form of the vitamin. Dogs can readily convert beta-carotene; however, cats must get their supply of vitamin A from a substance called *retinyl palmitate* or *retinol,* found only in animal sources. Feeding a complete and balanced cat food helps ensure that your cat receives adequate amounts of this fat-soluble vitamin necessary for normal vision, reproduction, and immune system function.

Because cats can store vitamin A in their livers, they do not need the nutrient replenished daily in their diets. In fact, an oversupply of vitamin A in the diet can lead to a toxic buildup in the tissues, causing skeletal deformities, weight loss, and even death. To prevent toxicity, avoid feeding a diet too rich in organ meats, particularly liver. Also,

avoid using cod-liver or other fish oils as routine, daily supplements, as these can lead to excessive accumulations of vitamins A and D (see page 75).

Vitamin A deficiencies are uncommon. Symptoms include retinal degeneration, corneal lesions, conjunctivitis, light sensitivity, weight loss, and a dull coat.

Vitamin D's primary function is to regulate the body's absorption of calcium and phosphorus. By doing so, this fat-soluble vitamin promotes strong bones and teeth. Often called the "sunshine vitamin," vitamin D is, in most mammals, including humans, synthesized in the skin following exposure to the ultraviolet rays from sunlight. However, studies suggest that cats do not effectively synthesize vitamin D in this way and must obtain the nutrient from their diet. In the wild, the bodies of small prey mammals readily supply enough vitamin D to satisfy a cat's normal needs.

In commercial cat foods, the animal-based ingredients, particularly fish and organ meats, provide a natural source of vitamin D. Canned foods tend to provide the highest levels. In addition, many pet foods are vitamin D-fortified. When added to food, the label usually lists it as *cholecalciferol* or *D-activated animal sterol.*

As with many other nutrients, too much can be just as bad as too little. Excessive supplementation of vitamin D can have damaging consequences, including hardening, or calcification, of the body's soft tissues and organs. A diet deficient in vitamin D can cause rickets in kittens and bone softening in adult cats. Some kittens with rickets develop enlarged joints, a bow-legged appearance, and soft bones prone to fracture easily. Deficiency signs can also include a reluctance to move, a short-stilted gait, and hind limb paralysis. Fortunately, deficiencies are rare, because commercial cat foods contain adequate amounts of this necessary vitamin.

Vitamin E, a fat-soluble vitamin also called *tocopherol,* enhances fertility, strengthens the immune system, and works with selenium as an antioxidant to help protect cells from damage due to oxidation. Tocopherol comes in several chemical forms found in egg yolk, dark green vegetables, wheat germ, and safflower and soybean oils. The alpha or active form is the dietary compound added to a food's nutrient mix, but other forms may also be used as preservatives to prevent fat rancidity in foods.

"Yellow fat disease" results from vitamin E deficiency and typically occurs in conjunction with a raw

Although cats love to nap in the sun, they don't readily synthesize the "sunshine" vitamin D in their skin the way humans and many other animals do. Instead, their diet must provide this important nutrient.

fish or an all-fish diet, particularly one too lavish in red tuna (see page 83). The concentrated amounts of unsaturated fatty acids in such diets destroy vitamin E.

Vitamin K is called *menadione* (in its synthetic form), *phylloquinone* (in its natural form), and sometimes just *vitamin K active substance.* The nutrient is found in green, leafy vegetables and functions as a clotting agent in the blood. Because cats can usually manufacture this fat-soluble vitamin on their own in sufficient amounts, deficiencies rarely occur, unless the cat undergoes extended treatment with antibiotics. Certain antibiotics readily destroy the intestinal bacteria that activate the internal production of vitamin K. A deficiency could cause abnormal bleeding and poor blood clotting ability. As with vitamin E, diets too high in fish may also interfere with vitamin K.

Vitamin C, also called *ascorbic acid*, is a water-soluble vitamin believed to be important in cell repair and in the production of collagen, a

substance that helps form the body's connective tissues. Vitamin C, found primarily in fruits and vegetables, also provides some immune system protection. For this reason, supplementation is believed by some to be useful during periods of stress or illness, although there is insufficient scientific data to support this theory. In any case, dietary supplementation of any kind should only be undertaken with the guidance of a veterinarian or animal nutrition expert. Because cats can synthesize vitamin C in their bodies, most cat foods are not fortified with it.

B-complex vitamins are critical in the proper metabolism of proteins, fats, and carbohydrates. Being water-soluble, excesses are excreted and not stored in the body.

Unlike the fat-soluble vitamins, most B vitamins must be replenished daily by the diet. Commercial pet foods typically add adequate amounts of B-complex vitamins to compensate for the predictable percentage that is destroyed by heat during the manufacturing process. Because the dietary sources of B-complex vitamins are similar—meats, wheat germ, brewer's yeast, egg yolk, milk, whole-grain cereals—a deficiency of one often means that others may be lacking as well.

Vitamin B1, also called *thiamine,* helps maintain normal weight, fitness, and nervous system function. Thiamine deficiency can be caused by feeding cats an exclusive diet of raw fish. Certain species of fish, such as carp and herring, contain an enzyme called thiaminase that destroys thiamine (see page 83). In humans, thiamine deficiency produces a disease called "beri-beri." In cats, a deficiency results in progressive stages of neurological disturbances, including appetite loss, weaving, circling, and inability to stand. Left untreated, thiamine deficiency can result in death.

Vitamin B2, also called *riboflavin,* is produced by intestinal bacteria in many animals. When added to foods, riboflavin rapidly deteriorates if exposed to light and stored improperly. A chronic deficiency may cause cataracts and other vision problems.

Vitamin B6, or *pyridoxine,* works with other dietary constituents to metabolize proteins and amino

Water-Soluble Vitamins: What They're Important For

B1 (thiamine)	Carbohydrate metabolism, normal neurologic function
B2 (riboflavin)	Cellular growth, normal vision, healthy skin
B6 (pyridoxine)	Protein and amino acid metabolism, kidney and urinary tract health
Niacin	Produces biochemical reactions that help the body use all major nutrients
Pantothenic acid	Carbohydrate, fat, and amino acid metabolism
Folacin (folic acid)	Normal growth and red blood cell production
Biotin	Necessary for certain biocehmical reactions during metabolism, health skin
B12 (cyanocobalamin)	Fat and carbohydrate metabolism
Choline	Moves fat from the liver and synthesizes the amino acid, methionine
Vitamin C (ascorbic acid)	Acts as an antioxidant, aids in cell repair

acids. Studies of B6-deficient cats have noted kidney damage and an increased presence of calcium oxalate crystals in the urinary tract with symptoms similar to those exhibited in FUS (feline urologic syndrome).

Vitamin B12 is often added to commercial cat foods in the form of *cyanocobalamin.* It contains the trace element cobalt. The vitamin is involved in the metabolism of fats and carbohydrates. The proper absorption of B12 depends on the ample supply of a protein called *intrinsic factor* in the intestines. A chronic condition called pernicious anemia results if this intrinsic factor is lacking.

Niacin is a B-complex vitamin that many animals can at least partially synthesize from the amino acid *tryptophan.* Cats, however, cannot do this as well and must get their daily allowance from the diet. Niacin is important for the proper synthesis of insulin and other hormones and for certain biochemical reactions necessary to free and use major nutrients from food. In humans, a niacin deficiency is called "pellagra." In cats, a deficiency is characterized by weight loss, diarrhea, loss of appetite, foul breath, mouth ulcers, excessive drooling, thickened saliva, and a red tongue. Left untreated, this deficiency rapidly causes death.

For proper digestion and metabolism, cats need a constant source of clean, fresh water.

in the cat's body (see page 83). For this reason, eggs should always be cooked before being fed to cats. Symptoms of biotin deficiency include hair loss, scaly skin, and weight loss.

Choline and inositol, components of lecithin, are not true vitamins. But they are important nutrients that work together to metabolize fats and help the liver eliminate wastes from the body. A deficiency can cause poor growth and an excessive accumulation of fat in the liver, also referred to as *fatty liver disease* or *hepatic lipidosis* (see page 94).

Pantothenic acid may be added to commercial cat foods as calcium pantothenate, but the cat's requirement for this B-complex vitamin is quite low. It works with other nutrients to help enhance immune system functions and to aid in the metabolism of carbohydrates, fats, and amino acids.

Folacin, or *folic acid*, is also important in immune system functions and in red blood cell production. Most of a cat's daily requirement is believed to be produced by normal bacteria present in the intestines. Folic acid deficiency results in weight loss and anemia.

Biotin helps keep the skin and coat healthy. An interesting aspect of this B-complex vitamin is that the enzyme *avidin* in raw egg whites renders it useless and unavailable

W Is for Water

Water, although sometimes the most overlooked and neglected nutrient, is perhaps the most important dietary element of all. It is more essential for survival than food. Animals have been known to subsist for weeks without food, but most cannot last for more than a few days without water. Water is fundamental to the digestion of food. In fact, digestion begins when enzymes secreted in water start dissolving food. This life-giving liquid is also a principle component of blood, transporting vital nutrients to the cells. Without water, the furnace, or nucleus, in the body's cells will not fire properly and perform the complex chemical reactions necessary to process and use nutrients at the cellular level.

Having evolved from desert animals, cats can conserve water efficiently. They can metabolize water from food and concentrate their urine to very high levels. But this ability doesn't mean that they can go more than a few days without drinking water before dehydration sets in. Cats can also become dehydrated if they lose too much water through their feces during bouts of diarrhea.

Because excessive amounts of minerals have been implicated as a cause of feline lower urinary tract disease, some people give their cats mineral-free bottled water as a precaution. While certainly not harmful, this expensive practice is not necessary, unless you happen to live in an area where the drinking water has an abnormally high mineral content. That being the case, the drinking water would probably not be the most desirable for human consumption either. Here's a good rule to follow: if the water isn't fit for you to drink, don't let your cat drink it.

The amount of water a cat needs varies with its age, health, and activity level. Climatic conditions and the kind of food a cat eats also influence water consumption. Canned cat food generally contains a moisture content of 78 percent or less. Dry and semimoist foods, of course, contain much less. Regardless of the type of food fed, always provide a plentiful source of clean, fresh water, preferably in a tip-proof bowl. Self-waterers, which dis-

Because thirsty cats will seek and find water on their own, make sure the available sources around your home are clean and not contaminated with insect larvae, plant fertilizers, pesticides, or other chemicals.

pense water into a bowl from an inverted bottle, are handy for multi-cat households and for times when you have to be away from home on an overnight trip.

Become familiar with your cat's drinking habits so you can report any noticeable change to your veterinarian. Excessive thirst and the ensuing frequent urination are symptoms of some serious disorders, such as diabetes and kidney failure, that require immediate medical attention.

Preservatives and Other Additives

Although many preservatives have little or no nutritional value, they are necessary components of cat food, because they prevent spoilage and

The antioxidant *ethoxyquin* is used in small amounts as a preservative in some pet foods. Besides preventing fat rancidity, studies indicate that the chemical may also protect against the poisonous effects of mold-induced mycotoxins, which can be a problem in some preservative-free foods. According to the Food and Drug Administration's Center for Veterinary Medicine (FDA-CVM), manufacturers are supposed to declare ethoxyquin on the label if a pet food contains it, regardless of whether they add the chemical directly or whether the ingredients they used came with the substance included. For example, fish meal is shipped with ethoxyquin (or BHA) already added as a preservative to keep the product stable. The label of a pet food that uses this material is also supposed to disclose the presence of the preservative.

Because of its classification as an insecticide for agricultural use, ethoxyquin has been the subject of much controversy. Although consumers have raised concerns about ethoxyquin allegedly causing cancer, thyroid disorders, reproductive failures, and other problems, repeated tests to date have not revealed any significant health risks associated with the amounts of ethoxyquin allowed in pet foods. Because of these consumer concerns, however, many pet food manufacturers have replaced ethoxyquin with the natural preservatives vitamin E (tocopherol) and vitamin C

extend the shelf life of products. They serve as antimicrobials or antioxidants, or both. As an antimicrobial, preservatives prevent the growth of harmful molds, yeasts, and bacteria in foods. As an antioxidant, preservatives prevent fats from becoming rancid. They do this by suppressing the reaction called oxidation that occurs when food combines with oxygen in the presence of light, heat, and some metals.

BHA (butylated hydroxyanisole), BHT (butylated hydroxytoluene), and ethoxyquin are common chemical preservatives added to fats in pet foods to prevent rancidity. Vitamin E (tocopherol) is a natural antioxidant widely used as a preservative to prevent fat rancidity. Rancid fats ruin the taste of the food and give off an unpleasant odor so that the cat is unlikely to eat. Rancidity can also damage essential amino acids and destroy important fat-soluble vitamins contained in the food. Not only does the food become unpleasant and unfit for consumption, it may even become toxic to the pet.

AAFCO Nutrient Profiles for Cat Foods

Nutrient	Units Dry Matter Basis	Growth & Repro. Minimum	Adult Maint. Minimum	Maximum
Protein	%	30.0	26.0	
Arginine	%	1.25	1.04	
Histidine	%	0.31	0.31	
Isoleucine	%	0.52	0.52	
Leucine	%	1.25	1.25	
Lysine	%	1.20	0.83	
Methionine-cystine	%	1.10	1.10	
Methionine	%	0.62	0.62	1.5
Phenylalanine-tyrosine	%	0.88	0.88	
Phenylalanine	%	0.42	0.42	
Threonine	%	0.73	0.73	
Tryptophan	%	0.25	0.16	
Valine	%	0.62	0.62	
Fat	%	9.0	9.0	
Linoleic acid	%	0.5	0.5	
Arachidonic acid	%	0.02	0.02	
Minerals				
Calcium	%	1.0	0.6	
Phosphorus	%	0.8	0.5	
Potassium	%	0.6	0.6	
Sodium	%	0.2	0.2	
Chloride	%	0.3	0.3	
Magnesium	%	0.08	0.04	
Iron	mg/kg	80	80	
Copper (extruded)	mg/kg	15	5	
Copper (canned)	mg/kg	5	5	
Manganese	mg/kg	7.5	7.5	
Zinc	mg/kg	75	75	2000.0
Iodine	mg/kg	0.35	0.35	
Selenium	mg/kg	0.1	0.1	
Vitamins				
Vitamin A	IU/kg	9000	5000	750000.0
Vitamin D	IU/kg	750	500	10000.0
Vitamin E	IU/kg	30	30	
Vitamin K	mg/kg	0.1	0.1	
Thiamine	mg/kg	5.0	5.0	
Riboflavin	mg/kg	4.0	4.0	
Pyridoxine	mg/kg	4.0	4.0	
Niacin	mg/kg	60	60	
Pantothenic acid	mg/kg	5.0	5.0	
Folic acid	mg/kg	0.8	0.8	
Biotin	mg/kg	0.07	0.07	
Vitamin B12	mg/kg	0.02	0.02	
Choline	mg/kg	2400	2400	
Taurine (extruded)	%	0.10	0.10	
Taurine (canned)	%	0.20	0.20	

Reprinted with permission from the Association of American Feed Control Officials, Inc., *1997 Official Publication*. (For ordering information, see Useful Addresses & Literature, page 148. Key: IU/kg = International Units per kilogram; mg/kg = milligrams per kilogram.

Preservatives are added to commercial cat foods to prolong shelf life and help prevent spoilage.

(ascorbic acid). However, products preserved with the latter two chemicals tend to have a somewhat shorter shelf life.

Another preservative *has* been removed from cat foods due to health concerns. When first introduced, semimoist foods contained *propylene glycol*, an ingredient used in cosmetics and alcoholic beverages. (Propylene glycol is also the main ingredient in "safer" antifreeze brands. See page 133.) The substance acted primarily as a humectant, preserving the moisture retention in the soft-dry foods. But when the chemical was implicated in causing red blood cell damage in cats, its use in cat foods was discontinued. Today, the more common preservatives used in semimoist foods to prevent mold and bacterial growth include sorbic acid and potassium sorbate. Glycerin is added as a humectant.

Other additives may provide artificial coloring or flavoring or act as vitamin and mineral sources. All chemical preservatives and non-

nutritive additives must be approved by the Food and Drug Administration (FDA) for use in pet foods. Any drug used in pet foods is also subject to FDA approval. To help ensure that they are harmless to pets, such substances must undergo required testing and meet certain criteria before approval for use is granted.

In general, artificial colors used in cat foods are the same ones approved for use in human foods. When used, colors are added for the human consumer's benefit rather than the cat's. Cats, of course, don't care what color their food is, as long as it tastes good. But for humans, these additives give products a more uniform, attractive appearance than the ingredients would provide in their natural state. Colors also help the human consumer differentiate between flavors in multiflavored foods. Because artificial colors have no nutritive value, foods without coloring, which are typically a flat, inconsistent gray or brown in appearance, are no more or less nutritious than identical products enhanced with colors. The following color additives have been used in pet foods: caramel, titanium dioxide, Red No. 40, Red No. 3, Yellow No. 5, Yellow No. 6, Blue No. 1, and Blue No. 2.

Flavoring agents make products more palatable to cats. Flavorings are either artificial ingredients with long chemical names, or they may be natural taste enhancers, such as brewer's yeast, garlic, and animal digests.

Chapter 3

Understanding Cat Foods and How They're Made

Today's Cat Food Market

Cats live longer, healthier lives today because of important advances in veterinary medicine and feline nutrition. As the popularity of the cat as a household pet has increased, so has consumer demand for better feline food products. This consumer interest, combined with continuing scientific advances in pet nutrition and veterinary medicine, has spurred many reputable pet food manufacturers to rethink and reformulate their products through the years. Gone are the old days when one product sufficed for both dogs and cats. Today, we know that cats cannot thrive on dog food alone. Our modern cat companions enjoy an unprecedented array of feline formulas geared to their special nutritional requirements at various stages of life, whether they're growing kittens, pregnant queens, nursing mothers, aging seniors, or ailing animals needing special feline prescription diets.

Aside from consumer demand, new cat food products typically undergo testing and must meet certain federal and state regulations before they can be shipped across state lines and offered for sale. Even so, many new products hit the shelves each year, giving human consumers an often overwhelming number of choices—from dry to semimoist to canned varieties, and from generic to supermarket to super-premium brands. At any one time, six to 12 *major* pet food manufacturers may vie for market shares and hundreds of different products come and go.

With so many choices available in today's market, it is relatively easy to find a product that your cat enjoys and that is convenient for you to serve. When selecting brands, however, it's important to remember that no one perfect food exists for every cat and every owner. Cats, like people, are individuals, and their individual nutritional needs can vary, depending on their activity level, weight, breed, environment, health status, and physical makeup. For example, many indoor cats lead a sedentary life, sleeping the hours away, while others allowed to roam outdoors expend more energy prowling their territory and hunting prey. In addition, an individual cat's nutritional needs change as the animal matures. Growing kittens need more protein and certain other nutrients than older cats. So, base your food choices not only on what your cat will eat, but also on what its stage of growth, age, and health status are.

Another important point to keep in mind is that most commercial cat foods are designed primarily to meet the needs of the *average* healthy cat. But some animals develop special needs that require special diets. (Refer also to the chapter Special

Use your cat's annual veterinary check-up to ask questions about nutrition and discuss its dietary needs with a professional.

Problems, Special Diets, on page 112). That's why, in addition to their commercial pet food lines, many major pet food companies have developed therapeutic diets, available through veterinarians. These are designed to manage an array of medical conditions from allergies to heart conditions and kidney disease. They are available through veterinarians because the nutrient content is specifically formulated for ailing or recovering felines. While these special, therapeutic diets usually meet feline maintenance requirements (see page 31), they may not in all cases provide an adequate mix of proteins, vitamins, and minerals for average, healthy cats, particularly ones in their growing or reproductive life stages.

Ultimately, the best gauge of any food's performance is your cat and how well it thrives and maintains ideal weight and condition on it. During your cat's annual checkup, your veterinarian can best judge whether your cat needs a dietary adjustment. Take this opportunity to discuss how and what you feed your cat, ask questions, and express any concerns you may have about recommended changes to your cat's diet. Your veterinarian and his or her staff are your best resources in your ongoing education as a responsible cat owner.

It's also important to know what the information on a cat food label means. The type and source of ingredients determines the overall quality of the food. Also, any

commercial pet food product that you intend to feed to your cat as its daily ration should say on the label that it provides *complete and balanced nutrition* for a specific life stage, as substantiated by accepted AAFCO protocols. In some cases, however, a claim of complete and balanced nutrition might mean that the food meets only the minimum standards necessary. There are some lower-quality foods on the market made from poorly digestible ingredients. The caring pet owner's challenge is to select nutritionally superior foods that help maximize an animal's chances of living a long and healthy life. Accomplishing this may require some investigation on the owner's part, such as calling manufacturers and asking about the nutrient content and the ingredient sources of their products. It also demands a basic understanding of the types of cat foods and what goes into them. (See also Choosing a Cat Food, page 55.)

Types of Cat Foods

Commercial cat foods come in three basic types: canned, dry, and semimoist, also called soft-moist or soft-dry. Each type of food has its advantages and disadvantages.

Canned foods contain more moisture; and often more meat (protein) and fat, than either dry or semimoist foods. According to AAFCO regulations, the moisture content in canned foods cannot exceed 78 percent, except for those that are liquid-based stews, gravies, broths,

sauces, or milk replacers. The higher moisture, protein, and fat content makes them generally more tasty to the feline consumer, which is probably why finicky eaters tend to snub everything that comes out of a bag or box and hold out for the canned goods. On the downside, canned foods are usually more expensive to buy (you're actually paying for the water, too) than dry or semimoist foods, especially the so-called "gourmet" varieties. Incidentally, the term *gourmet* has no regulated meaning in the industry and does not necessarily mean that the food adheres to any higher standard of quality or taste.

When feeding canned foods, always take up the leftovers as soon as the cat finishes eating. This prevents spoilage. A common problem with canned food is getting the cat to eat the leftover portion at the next meal after it has been refrigerated. Evolution seems to have conditioned felines to prefer their meals

While there may be hundreds of cat food flavors and varieties on the market, the three basic types are canned, dry, and semimoist.

Most canned foods come with easy-to-open pop-top lids. Once opened, leftover portions must be put in a resealable, airtight container and stored in the refrigerator.

slightly warm, or at approximately the body temperature of small mammals of prey. For this reason, always bring chilled food to room temperature before serving. If you warm it in a microwave or on a stovetop, test it with your finger first to make sure it isn't too hot to serve. Also, when refrigerating leftovers, remove the unused portion from the can and store it in an airtight, covered container. This prevents the food from taking on the can's metallic taste and from absorbing other refrigerated food odors, factors that also may contribute to the cat's refusal of the food at the next meal.

Sealed canned goods have a nearly indefinite shelf life, but rusted cans or ones with bulging lids should be discarded, contents and all. Avoid the dented cans at the grocery store, too, as these may have tiny pinholes that let in air to spoil the contents. Likewise, discard foods that smell rancid or look molded when opened, or when possible, take them back to the store for exchange. (Take care to wrap and discard ruined foods in such a way that your cat or other neighborhood animals will not get into the garbage and consume something that will make them sick.) Although some canned foods still require a can opener, many manufacturers have redesigned their products with convenient pop-top lids.

Dry foods: Generally, dry foods are less expensive and more convenient for the owner to serve. Plus, there are no smelly cans to go in the trash can. Measured portions of dry foods can be left out all day in a bowl for cats to nibble at will (called free-choice feeding, a method many cats prefer), whereas canned foods spoil readily when left out too long. Typically sold by the bag, box, or plastic jug, dry foods have a long shelf life, usually between nine months and one year, depending on what preservatives are used. Some products preserved with tocopherols (vitamin E) may have a somewhat shorter shelf life. Most manufacturers post a "Best If Used By" date on the bag. A bag of good-quality dry food should not contain an excessive amount of fine crumbs in the bottom, nor should the bag look or feel greasy on the outside.

In addition to their cost and convenience, dry foods may help maintain better dental health in cats, because the hard chewing action scours the teeth and gums. Just how much dry foods contribute to feline dental health remains a matter of debate because most cats tend to chew only a few times before bolting down the pieces whole. Still, the dental factor may make dry foods a better choice for certain breeds prone to gingivitis (gum inflammation), such as Somalis, Abyssinians, Persians, and Exotic Shorthairs, among others. Why some breeds appear to be more prone to gum disease than others is unclear, although the problem may be related to mouth size and jaw alignment.

Because the greater protein and fat content of canned foods makes them generally more palatable to cats, owners often find it difficult to switch a cat's diet from canned to dry foods. Cats develop taste preferences early in life, and once set they can be quite difficult to change, even if the cat's health depends on it. To avoid ever having to grapple with this finicky behavior, simply offer a variety of food types, textures, and flavors from kittenhood on. Of course, this doesn't mean you have to buy a different kind of food every week. Even within the same brand, there's generally enough variety of both type and flavors for you to pick two or three your cat seems to like and rotate them on a regular basis.

A typical routine for many owners involves feeding canned portions at one meal and leaving out an appropriate amount of dry rations for free-choice nibbling

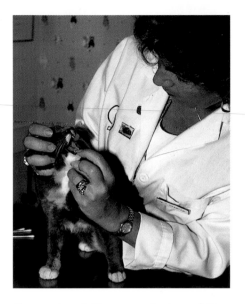

While dry foods may contribute minimally to better feline dental health, they are no substitute for regular dental check-ups and professional cleanings.

throughout the remainder of the day. This method is acceptable as long as you're careful not to overfeed, thus encouraging the cat to overeat and gain weight. If your cat does gain too much weight, you may need to gradually cut down on the amount fed or abandon free-choice feeding in favor of controlled portions offered only at set mealtime intervals. Before implementing any kind of weight-loss program for an obviously overweight cat, consult your veterinarian first and have the cat examined for underlying health problems that may be contributing to the condition. (Refer also to the chapter on "Obesity: Making Fat Cats Fit," page 86.)

At one time, it was thought that letting cats nibble on dry foods throughout the day predisposed them to feline urologic syndrome (FUS), a potentially fatal urinary

This heaping bowl of food may be far more than this cat needs to eat in one day. To feed the proper amount, consult the product feeding guidelines and measure out the recommended daily ration.

tract obstruction. This was attributed partly to a higher magnesium content in dry food and partly to significant amounts of vegetable-based ingredients that made the urine pH too alkaline. Since that time, however, most major brands have been reformulated, with acidifying ingredients added to help maintain urine pH levels safely within normal acidic ranges (see page 16). Some ingredients that tend to make the diet, and consequently the urine, slightly more acidic include corn gluten meal, animal digest, phosphoric acid, methionine, poultry meal, and certain animal proteins. Nowadays, the feeding guidelines of many commercial dry foods that contain acidifying ingredients recommend pouring a measured amount, either per meal or per day, in a bowl and leaving it for the cat to eat free-choice

or at will. In fact, studies have shown that feline urine tends to become more alkaline following a big meal eaten all at once, whereas a feeding pattern consisting of smaller, more frequent meals seems to decrease this tendency. The free-choice method also allows cats, who are true nibblers at heart, to follow a more natural schedule of eating 10 or more small meals throughout the day.

Semimoist foods: These soft-moist, nugget-shaped foods attempt to combine some benefits of the dry and canned forms, making these products convenient for the human consumer to use. Compared to dry diets, semimoist foods generally offer higher palatability for the feline consumer. They also contain more moisture than dry foods, but not as much as canned foods. They are usually packaged in foil pouches for single serving meals. But this convenience packaging makes them more expensive to buy than dry foods. The larger foil-lined bags are more comparable in price to dry foods.

Some manufacturers make a distinction between foods that are semimoist and soft-dry; however, the main difference seems to be the moisture content. Semimoist foods have a somewhat higher moisture content than soft-dry foods. Also, the soft-dry foods offer a combination of dry and soft textures.

Like dry rations, semimoist and soft-dry foods can be left out and fed free-choice without spoiling, and they are not as smelly as canned foods. Also like dry rations, semimoist foods have a long shelf life, but if stored too long, the nuggets turn hard and become dry and powdery and should be discarded. On the down side, semimoist products, unlike dry foods, are too soft to help reduce tartar and provide no benefit to feline dental health. Semimoist foods also tend to contain more sugar (corn syrup), artificial colors, and chemical preservatives. Originally, these products contained a chemical preservative called *propylene glycol*. When this preservative was implicated in causing red blood cell damage in cats, responsible cat food manufacturers removed it from their products. The substance is no longer allowed for use in cat foods.

Classifications of Cat Foods

Manufacturers market cat foods as generic (economy), popular (supermarket brands), premium, or super-premium brands. The characteristics of products in these categories can vary widely from one manufacturer to another.

Economy or generic brands: Foods in this category are usually sold under a feed or grocery store chain's name as opposed to a nationally advertised brand name. Generics are designed to offer similar guarantees and ingredients to name-brand products, but at a lower price. Their cheaper price often means that they are made of the least expensive (and lowest quality) ingredients available, but this is not always the case. The lower cost is also often due to the fact that fewer advertising dollars are spent marketing these products. Sometimes it is more cost-effective for a manufacturer to simply slap a generic label on one of its regular products and market it for a lower price as an economy brand, instead of remixing the formula. In general, however, you get what you pay for with cat food, as with most other consumer goods. Comparative studies have shown that some generic brands use poorer-grade ingredients, have lower energy values, and are less digestible. An animal has to eat more of a poorly digestible food to extract adequate nutrient value from the contents. In terms of quantity consumed, this can actually cost you more. Certainly, economy brands demand a bit more investigation by the consumer to determine whether adequate nutritional standards went into the manufacturing of the product.

Popular or regular brands: These are the nationally advertised name brand foods sold in supermarkets that people are most familiar with. They cost more than generic brands, but usually not as much as the premium or super-premium foods sold primarily though pet supply stores. Compared to economy brands, popular brands

For optimum health and growth, feed your kittens the highest quality cat food you can afford.

tend to contain better-quality ingredients and are more digestible. These formulas are often well researched and designed to meet the nutritional needs of the average cat at specified life stages.

Premium and super-premium foods: Although certain brands of the more expensive premium cat foods are being marketed in grocery stores with increasing frequency, many are still sold primarily through wholesale distributors, pet supply stores, and some veterinary clinics. Despite this marketing strategy, some popular and premium brands may actually differ very little, except for price. This is because the terms *premium* and *super-pre-*

mium are really just marketing tools and have no official, regulated meaning in the industry. The general assumption, however, is that premium foods remain stable in their makeup, whereas popular brands are more likely to change recipe ingredients according to the current market cost and availability of those ingredients. It is also generally assumed that because premium brands cost more, they contain higher-quality ingredients, and that super-premium foods contain the highest grade ingredients. While these assumptions may hold true for many fine products on the market, it is important for consumers to be aware that cat food products marketed under these superlatives may not necessarily contain any special or higher-quality ingredients and are not required to measure up to any higher standard of nutrition. Although the words *premium* and *super-premium* imply higher quality, different manufacturers interpret and apply these terms differently. This means that the characteristics of foods classified as such may be inconsistent from one manufacturer to another. If you have doubts or questions about a particular product, call the manufacturer's toll-free number and ask for specific information about nutrient content and sources of ingredients.

Cost does indicate quality in some cases. Many premium foods are designed to be highly digestible, which means that the cat actually requires less of it in terms of quantity, since more nutrients (and usually more calories) can be readily absorbed, metabolized, and utilized from smaller servings. They are also designed to be power-packed with nutrition. The amount of each nutrient in relation to how much of the food can actually be metabolized for energy is what is meant by the terms *nutrient-dense* and *energy-dense,* often used interchangeably to describe many premium foods. Greater digestibility of these nutrients also means less waste, which translates to smaller stool volume in the litter box. In fact, the best way to determine how well your cat seems to be digesting a particular food is to note how much is coming out the other end. Large, bulky stools indicate poor digestibility.

While high-protein, nutrient-dense, premium foods are excellent choices for growing kittens and pregnant or nursing queens with greater energy requirements, more sedentary adult cats may grow fat on such a rich diet, especially if the amounts fed are not carefully controlled. In general, the better the quality of the food, the less quantity it takes to feed, because of the power-packed nutrient content. But if a cat has been used to eating larger quantities of a lesser-quality food, and especially if it tends to overeat anyway, abruptly switching to a premium brand can result in weight gain if you don't pay particular attention to the amounts fed and adjust them accordingly. For a start, follow the feeding guidelines on package labels. Also, remember to make all changes in diet gradually.

Therapeutic diets are available through veterinarians. Many people commonly refer to these products as prescription diets; however, veterinarians do not prescribe these foods in the same fashion that medications are prescribed for humans. Therefore, the preferred term for products of this genre is therapeutic diet. This latter term is actually a more apt description, because these diets are designed to be dispensed for the medical management of cats with special needs due to heart disease, kidney dysfunction, intestinal disorders, obesity, or other health problems. While most therapeutic diets come in dry or canned form, at least one used for recurrent gastrointestinal problems is available in soft-moist nuggets.

Natural cat foods: While not in a classification of their own, *natural* cat foods have become the trendy diet of the 90s, spurred by health-conscious owners who want only the best for their beloved feline charges. Unfortunately, *natural* means something different to everybody—especially among pet food manufacturers. Like the term *premium,* the word *natural* has no regulated meaning in the industry at this time and is mostly a marketing tool. AAFCO is currently considering a proposal for establishing a new guideline with regard to what can or cannot be included in a product for it to bear the claim of *natural* on the label.

Because *natural* implies that the product is in some way healthier or more wholesome, these products often cost more than standard commercial cat foods. But do you really get your money's worth? Maybe. Maybe not. There are no controlled studies that definitively prove that so-called natural products are any better than the standard fare. At present, the issue really depends on owner or buyer preference. Some makers of these products claim to use only whole ingredients instead of byproducts. Many stake their *natural* claim on the way the food is preserved, using natural substances such as vitamins E and C as preservatives (called "mixed tocopherols") instead of chemical preservatives such as ethoxyquin. While much controversy has surrounded the use of ethoxyquin in pet foods, studies have repeatedly shown the substance to be safe in low levels. It is also an extremely effective, long-lasting preservative; whereas products preserved with tocopherols have a somewhat shorter shelf life. Still, many owners object to the idea of feeding their pets chemicals and are willing to pay the difference.

How Cat Foods Are Made

The Extrusion Process

Cat foods are cooked and sterilized to kill any harmful microorganisms originating from the slaughtered carcasses or from other processing sources. In the case of dry and semimoist cat foods, the ingredient mixture is steamed and pressure-cooked in a machine called an extruder. An extruder is a large cylindrical channel with a screw, called an auger, that spins the channel and mixes the ingredients. The opening in the die cap of the extruder can be designed to almost any shape, depending on how the manufacturer wants the finished product to look. When the cooked batter is squeezed through the die cap, it is molded into the desired shape and cut into bite-size pieces. At this point, dry foods may be coated with digests, vegetable oil, dry milk, beef tallow, or flavor enhancers for greater palatability.

Although special shapes are designed primarily to attract the attention of the human consumer, they are planned with the feline consumer in mind as well. Cats, of

In the extrusion process, the raw ingredients of dry cat foods are cooked at a high temperature for a short time. The rotating screw moves the mixture toward the die, where the food is cut to a specific size and shape.

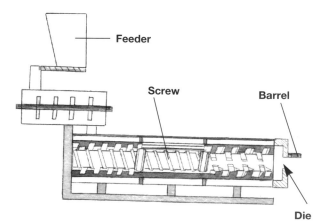

Feeder

Screw

Barrel

Die

course, don't care whether their food is shaped like tiny fish. But they do seem to care about how the food particles feel in their mouth. *Mouth feel*, as this factor is known in the industry, is an important consideration in the product design of any cat food, because it contributes to the overall palatability and pleasantness of the food. If you've ever wondered why dry cat foods come in so many different shapes, it's because preference studies using live test animals have shown that mouth feel can be influenced by the shape, texture, density, and size of the food particles.

Special die caps produce the different shapes of cat foods during the extrusion process. Colorings and flavorings are generally sprayed on afterward.

Canning

Canned cat foods are made in a process that is similar to home-canning methods. Water is added to the base ingredient mixture. The mix is then brought to a certain temperature and loaded into cans. After the cans are sealed, the food is pressure-cooked in the can. This process kills any bacteria present in the food material.

Quality Control

Pet food manufacturing plants are subject to outside inspections by the Food and Drug Administration (FDA) and state regulatory agencies. Inspectors can examine plant records and all phases of production to help ensure that pet foods are being labeled and shipped in compliance with the appropriate regulations. Because of limited personnel and resources, these agencies tend to focus their regulatory efforts on the larger manufacturers.

For this reason, most manufacturers enforce elaborate quality control measures on incoming and outgoing products. For example, reputable pet food manufacturers take steps to limit the occurrence of hair in their products. Although there is no evidence that hair found in cat food is harmful to cats, some human consumers find it objectionable. Meat packing houses remove hair from animal carcasses, but minimal amounts of hair may show up in their shipments intended for pet food, even when good processing practices are observed. Responsible manufacturers enforce routine inspections and quality control measures to help ensure that the packing house shipments they accept do not contain excessive amounts of hair and other undesirable materials. They also check incoming heat-processed ingredients for signs of charring or burning, as these factors can adversely affect a food's flavor and nutrient availability. While pressure cooking certainly does not eliminate the presence of hair, the heat sterilization removes any health risk that may be associated with hair.

Packaging

As one might expect, dry and semimoist foods are packaged assembly-line fashion. The kibble is poured into bags, jugs, or foil pouches and sealed with sophisticated machinery that automates much of the process. Vacuum packaging is a completely different technology, and because of its expense it is used by only a few manufacturers. Simply put, the process involves adding a gas as the product is being put into the package. This gas somehow displaces the air so that there is no air left in the package when it is sealed. The advantages of this technology are twofold. First, it condenses the size of the package by removing the air, a feature that allows more product to be displayed on less shelf space. Also, because it removes air from around the product, vacuum packaging can improve shelf life and help preserve the nutrient quality longer.

How Cat Food Is Tested

Responsible manufacturers continually rely on scientific research and testing protocols to help them develop new or improved products. Although each manufacturer has its own procedure for developing a new product or for changing an existing one, all develop market prototypes and test their products in various ways. Besides being test-fed to animals to determine nutritional adequacy and overall taste preference, a food may be subjected to storage tests for as long as one year. Altogether, it can take two or more years to develop and test a new product before it finally ends up on the market. Common tests used to evaluate new or improved cat food products include:

Palatability Studies

No matter how nutritious a food may be, it is of no use to the cat if the cat won't eat it. Palatability studies help determine whether a product appeals to the feline taste buds. In a controlled study, cats

Cats don't care about the color of their food, but research has shown that they do care about texture and mouth feel. That's why dry foods come in so many different shapes.

are offered ample amounts of two different foods at the same time, in the same size bowls. Because some cats grow accustomed to eating from only the right or the left bowl, researchers switch the bowls' positions daily. The cats' apparent preference between the two choices of foods is noted and evaluated over a period of time.

Palatability is influenced as much by the ingredient mix as by the quality of the ingredients. Burned, overcooked, or rancid ingredients are no more appealing to pets than they are to people. As previously discussed, mouth feel also is an important consideration. Just as many people detest corn flakes that turn soggy in milk, cats appear to dislike dry foods that turn to mush when moisture is added. In fact, tests have shown that cats seem to prefer dry foods that have a crunchy texture.

Storage Tests

Manufacturers may store foods for periods of three months to a year to determine whether the nutrient values and palatability of the product will change over time under typical storage conditions. In some cases, various climatic conditions are simulated to determine what effects, if any, extreme humidity and other weather conditions may have on the product during shipping and storage.

Nutritional Studies

To state on a label that a cat food provides "complete and balanced"

nutrition, based on AAFCO's requirements, a manufacturer must be able to prove this claim either by formulating the product to meet an AAFCO Cat Food Nutrient Profile (which can be achieved by calculation) or by test feeding the product to cats of the appropriate age or life cycle. Actual feeding trials may be the most expensive and time-consuming way to prove this claim, but they offer greater assurance that a new or improved product meets adequate nutritional guidelines. To substantiate a cat food's nutritional adequacy through animal feeding trials, manufacturers follow AAFCO's established feeding protocols, which are detailed in that agency's *Official Publication*. These protocols outline the manner in which feeding trials are to be conducted so that the basis for substantiating nutritional claims is consistent throughout the industry.

Reproduction Studies

These tests are designed to substantiate that a new or improved product adequately meets the nutritional needs of pregnant and nursing female cats. The tests start before breeding and end after weaning of the kittens. Two groups of females are used. One group receives the test diet, while the other is fed a control diet that already has been proven to support normal reproduction. A veterinarian examines all of the animals, and technicians monitor their body weights and measure their blood chemistry values routinely. Any

Cat foods formulated for "all life stages" can be fed to kittens and pregnant or nursing queens because they meet the standards accepted for growth and reproduction as outlined in the AAFCO protocols.

changes in health or appearance are recorded and scrutinized. At the end of the study, the test diet's performance must be as good as or better than the control diet.

Growth Studies

Because kittens grow rapidly during their first year, they, like pregnant and nursing queens, need special nutrition to support their extra energy needs. Growth tests help determine whether a product can adequately meet these special needs and support normal growth after weaning. Similar to reproduction studies, growth studies use two groups of kittens. One receives the test diet, while the other gets a proven control diet. Similar observations are recorded, and at the study's end the test diet passes if it equals or exceeds the performance of the control diet.

If a product passes both the reproduction and the growth stud-

ies, it can rightfully bear the label claim of "complete and balanced nutrition for all life stages." This means the food can be fed to cats of all ages.

Maintenance Studies

These tests help determine whether a product can maintain normal health in adult cats not used for breeding. For a minimum of 26 weeks, a group of cats at least one year of age or older receive the test diet. Their blood chemistry profiles are measured, and their overall physical condition is evaluated routinely. The test diet passes if no animals lose substantial weight or condition during this time. The product can then be labeled as providing "complete and balanced nutrition for maintenance of the adult cat." It is important to note that a product labeled as such does not meet the extra nutritional needs of growing kittens or pregnant and nursing queens, and therefore should not be fed to animals in growth or reproductive life stages. This is because adult, nonbreeding cats typically do not require the additional protein, vitamins, and minerals needed for growth, gestation, and lactation; therefore, products designed solely for adult maintenance can contain lower nutrient levels than products intended for growth and reproduction or for all life stages.

Digestibility Studies

Not all energy or nutrients in a food can be used by the animal that eats it. A certain amount always ends up as waste, which is why you have to scoop out the litter box each day. The nutritional value of a food, as measured in *digestibility,* refers to the percentage of total nutrients actually digested, absorbed, and made available to the cat for use when the food is eaten. During digestion studies, fecal material is collected and analyzed for nutrient content. Digestibility is then calculated by subtracting the amount of a particular nutrient found in the fecal matter from the total amount known to be in the food consumed. Not all pet food companies conduct digestion studies, but those that do will usually send you the information, along with a nutrient analysis, if you call the toll-free telephone number on the package and request it.

Higher digestibility means that the cat absorbs and uses more of what it eats. But digestibility information is not disclosed on cat food labels. The *crude protein* amount required in a label's guaranteed analysis is only an estimated minimum percentage of the nutrient, not the actual amount available to or used by the cat. In fact, it's possible for a product with a higher guarantee of crude protein to actually deliver less usable protein to the animal if the food contains less digestible ingredients. A product's digestibility is influenced not only by the mixture and quality of ingredients, but also by the methods used to cook and process them.

What's in Cat Food?

Byproducts of the human food industry: Many cat food varieties list "meat byproducts" or "poultry byproducts" on the label as primary ingredients. While some pet food manufacturers claim to use only products that would be deemed suitable for human consumption, the term *byproducts* generally refers to cuts of meat or parts of animals not typically used for human consumption. Rather than wasting these byproducts of the human food industry, meat-packing houses sell them to manufacturers that use them to make pet foods. Depending on the specific feed ingredient, such parts may include the lungs, kidneys, livers, stomachs, intestines, brains, blood, and bone (but not hair, horns, hooves, or teeth) left over from slaughtered animal carcasses. In the case of poultry, byproducts may include the heads, viscera, necks, and feet of chickens or turkeys. When the word *meal* is

Diets designed for the maintenance of adult cats are not suitable fare for active, growing kittens.

While some people may grimace at cat food contents, it's important to remember that, under wild conditions, birds, rodents, and other small animals— usually eaten whole—make up the natural feline diet.

cats evolved as predators, which means that their diet in the wild consists mainly of birds, rodents, and other small animals, usually eaten whole, including heads, feet, bones, skin, fur, feathers, internal organs, entrails, bowel contents, as well as any partially digested vegetable or insect matter in the stomachs of the prey. Moreover, cats subsisted for thousands of years on this raw, wild-caught diet without the benefit of the heat processing and sterilization methods used in today's pet food industry to destroy potentially harmful bacteria and parasites.

Plant protein: Most cat food formulas supplement animal protein sources with plant protein sources, such as brewer's rice, ground corn, and wheat flour. Cereal grains provide important sources of bulk fiber and carbohydrate energy. Some plant proteins are also byproducts. For example, soybean meal is a byproduct of soybean oil production, and corn gluten meal is dried corn residue left after the whole starch is removed to make corn starch or syrup. Middlings, a byproduct of flour milling, are a source of crude fiber. Beet pulp, also a source of fiber in pet foods, is a byproduct of sugar beets used in sugar production.

used after an animal byproduct, as in "poultry byproduct meal," this means the feed ingredient has been ground and rendered from such parts. To prevent byproducts intended for pet foods from being mistaken for human food, they are sometimes marked with colored dye or charcoal, which usually breaks down during processing.

Animal protein: Although consuming the heads, feet, and intestines of chickens may sound thoroughly disgusting and unappetizing to some cat owners, these parts and other meat byproducts contribute vital animal protein and amino acids to the feline diet. Besides, they more closely mimic a natural diet than some highly processed "people" foods. After all,

Additives: Vitamins, minerals, and other important nutrients are added to the cat food formula as necessary to supplement those derived from the natural ingredients or to compensate for predictable nutrient losses that may occur during normal processing and storage. Pet food makers typically buy these nutrients in a prepared mix ready to add to their manufacturing process. Because a cat's body cannot, in most cases, distinguish between synthetic vitamins and those that occur naturally in the primary ingredients, synthetic nutrients are frequently added to achieve a higher degree of nutritional quality and balance. These added nutrients have to be listed on the label, and they're easily recognized by their chemical-sounding names that usually end with something such as *nitrate, chloride,* or *sulfate.* One example of a commonly used synthetic mineral is *ferrous sulfate*, a high-potency form of iron.

Non-nutritional additives include preservatives, flavor enhancers, and artificial colors. While these ingredients may not provide additional nutrient benefits, they do serve a specific purpose in the food formula (see page 29).

Feed ingredient definitions: AAFCO's *Official Publication* contains an extensive list of feed ingredient definitions that manufacturers conform to in labeling their products. Here are just a few feed ingredients that may appear on pet food labels and their official definitions:

- **Meat** is the clean flesh derived from slaughtered mammals and is limited to that part of the striate muscle that is skeletal or that matter found in the tongue, in the diaphragm, in the heart, or in the

esophagus; with or without the accompanying and overlying fat and the portions of the skin, sinew, nerve, and blood vessels that normally accompany the flesh. It shall be suitable for use in animal food. If it bears a name descriptive of its kind (e.g., beef, pork, poultry), it must correspond thereto.

- **Meat byproducts** are the non-rendered (not ground up and processed), clean parts, other than meat, derived from slaughtered mammals. It includes, but is not limited to, lungs, spleen, kidneys, brain, livers, blood, bone, partially defatted low temperature fatty tissue, and stomachs and intestines freed of their contents. It does not include hair, horns, teeth, and hooves. It shall be suitable for use in animal food. If it bears a name descriptive of its kind, it must correspond thereto. (AAFCO's Pet Food Regulations further stipulate that "the terms *meat* and *meat byproducts* shall

Complete and balanced nutrition is key to the health of domestic house cats, who depend on humans for all their needs. Many cat foods have synthetic nutrients added to enhance nutritional quality and balance.

be qualified to designate the animal from which the meat and meat byproducts are derived unless the meat and meat byproducts are from cattle, swine, sheep and goats." For example, if the meat or meat byproducts come from horse, they must be qualified as *horse meat* and *horse meat byproducts*.)

- **Meat and bone meal** is the rendered product from mammal tissues, including bone, exclusive of any added blood, hair, hoof, horn, hide trimmings, manure, stomach and rumen contents, except in such amounts as may occur unavoidably in good processing practices. (The term *rendered* means the tissues have been ground up and cooked at high temperature to remove moisture and separate the protein and fat.) Meat and bone meal shall not contain added extraneous materials not provided for in this definition. It shall contain a minimum of 4 percent phosphorus, and the calcium level shall not be more than 2.2 times the actual phosphorus level. It shall not contain more than 12 percent pepsin indigestible residue, and not more than 9 percent of the crude protein in the product shall be pepsin indigestible. The label shall include guarantees for minimum crude protein, minimum crude fat, maximum crude fiber, minimum phosphorus, and minimum and maximum calcium. If it bears a name descriptive of its kind, com-position, or origin, it must correspond thereto.

- **Poultry meal** is the dry rendered product from a combination of clean flesh and skin with or without accompanying bone, derived from the parts of whole carcasses of poultry or a combination thereof, exclusive of feathers, heads, feet, and entrails. It shall be suitable for use in animal food. If it bears a name descriptive of its kind, it must correspond thereto.

- **Fish meal** is the clean, dried, ground tissue of undecomposed whole fish or fish cuttings, either or both, with or without the extraction of part of the oil. It must contain not more than 10 percent moisture. If it contains more than 3 percent salt, the amount of salt must constitute a part of the brand name, provided that in no case must the salt content of this product exceed 7 percent.

- **Animal digest** is material that results from chemical and enzymatic hydrolysis of clean and undecomposed animal tissue. The animal tissues used shall be exclusive of hair, horns, teeth, hooves, and feathers, except in trace amounts as might occur unavoidably in good factory practice, and shall be suitable for animal feed. If it bears a name descriptive of its kind or flavors, it must correspond thereto. (Liquid or powdered digests are often used to coat dry foods to improve flavor.)

- **Animal fat** is obtained from the tissues of mammals and poultry in the commercial processes of rendering or extracting. It consists predominantly of glyceride esters of fatty acids and contains no additions of free fatty acids or other materials obtained from fats. It must contain, and be guaranteed for, not less than 90 percent total fatty acids, not more than 2.5 percent unsaponifiable (unconvertible) matter, and not more than 1 percent insoluble impurities. Maximum free fatty acids and moisture must also be guaranteed. If the product bears a name descriptive of its kind or origin, it must correspond thereto. If an antioxidant is used, the common name or names must be indicated, followed by the words "used as a preservative."
- **Ground corn** is the entire corn kernel ground or chopped. It must contain not more than 4 percent foreign material. May also appear in the ingredient list of a mixed feed as corn meal or corn chop.
- **Brewer's rice** is the small fragments of rice kernels that have been separated from the larger kernels of milled rice.
- **Feeding oat meal** is obtained in the manufacture of rolled oat groats or rolled oats and consists of broken oat groats, oat groat chips, and floury portions of the oat groats, with only such quantity of finely ground oat hulls as is unavoidable in the usual process

of commercial milling. It must not contain more than 4 percent crude fiber.
- **Dried kelp** is dried seaweed of the families *Laminariacae* and *Fucaeae*. The maximum percentage of salt and the minimum percentage of potassium must be declared. If the kelp is sold as a source of iodine, the minimum percentage of iodine must be declared. If the product is prepared by artificial drying, it may be called "dehydrated kelp."

(This partial list of definitions is reprinted with permission from AAFCO's 1996 Official Publication. The book contains an extended list of official feed ingredient definitions used in pet and livestock foods. For ordering information, see Addresses and Useful Literature in the back of this book.)

To meet the extra demands placed on kittens' active, growing bodies, AAFCO recommends that at least 30 percent of their diet be comprised of protein.

Use of Horse Meat in Cat Food

Except for certain formulas designed primarily for big cats housed in zoos, horse meat is not widely used in commercial cat foods in the United States. This is largely due to a cultural aversion to horse meat consumption in this country. In parts of Europe, however, the practice is more accepted. When horse meat is used in products marketed in the United States, it must, according to AAFCO's guidelines, be clearly designated as such on the label. Because the terms *meat* and *meat byproducts* can apply only to cattle, swine, sheep, and goats, material from any other source must be qualified on the label as to the animal of origin. This means that, if a food's contents are derived from horses, the label should state *horse meat* or *horse byproducts*, according to AAFCO's Official Pet Food Regulations. Similarly, if the meat or meat byproducts in a cat food are composed of venison or rabbit (neither of which is widely used in the United States), the label should declare the animal of origin.

Use of Rendered Animals

The term *rendered* means that the tissues of animals have been ground up and cooked at high temperature to remove moisture and separate the protein and fat. The process destroys most common bacteria, viruses, and parasites, so that the end product is, in most cases, generally deemed safe for use in animal feeds. The end products of this process can be used for many other purposes as well.

The majority of rendered material that is turned into suitable animal feed ingredients comes from the byproducts of animals slaughtered for human food, because that is what is most readily available in the marketplace. Such ingredients include poultry meal and poultry byproduct meal, both commonly used in cat foods. Other animals that have died or been destroyed or that have died on their way to slaughter may also be rendered and used to produce fertilizers, industrial lubricants, animal feeds, and similar products. In the industry, this latter group is referred to as the 4-Ds—dead, dying, diseased, or disabled animals. While the idea may seem distasteful to some, rendering serves as a useful recycling function in today's society.

Years ago, however, articles began appearing about the use of so-called 4-D animals, as well as euthanized companion animals, in rendered products, raising some unsettling questions about whether materials from either source eventually find their way into commercial pet foods and, if so, whether consumers should be concerned about this practice. While some rendered material from 4-D livestock may wind up in some pet food products, it is very unlikely that euthanized companion animals meet that end, although the possibility certainly exists. How could this happen?

Here's what occurs in the industry. In larger cities, some animal control facilities, faced with economic or environmental restraints that limit their disposal options, contract with rendering plants to rid themselves of the massive numbers of cats and dogs they must euthanize every year. Conceivably, these animals may be mixed and rendered with various other 4-D mammals to be turned into end products for industrial uses. However, the likelihood that any significant amount of material rendered from companion animals would ever wind up in cat food is minimal, according to the Food and Drug Administration's Center for Veterinary Medicine (FDA-CVM).

For one thing, the experts say, most pet food manufacturers, mindful of the effects of unfavorable publicity on their sales, are careful to specify the source of their ingredients. For example, when they order raw materials from their suppliers, they can specify that the source be solely from beef or poultry to ensure that they receive rendered material that is, for example, exclusively *poultry meal* or *beef meal*, which is then reflected on the product's label.

But one feed ingredient, *meat and bone meal*, seems particularly vulnerable to the possibility of containing this material. While *meat and bone meal* is not all that common on cat food ingredient lists, it is an accepted and inexpensive source of protein and minerals in animal feeds. Unlike *meat* and *meat byproducts*, the origin of *meat and bone meal* is not limited to specific types of animals. As previously discussed, the terms *meat* and *meat byproducts* are strictly regulated by AAFCO to

mean that either of these ingredients can be derived only from slaughtered cattle, swine, sheep, or goats, unless stated otherwise (as in *horse meat* or *horse byproducts*). But *meat and bone meal*—although usually derived mostly from pork because of its market prevalence—means simply rendered or ground up *mammal tissues*, including bone, but excluding hair, hooves, horn, and so on. (See the section on feed ingredient definitions, page 50.) And, unless otherwise described on the label, these mammal tissues do not necessarily have to be from slaughtered animals or from any specific origin. This opens the way for a small percentage of the mammal tissue to conceivably come from euthanized cats and dogs or from animals other than those slaughtered for food.

Aside from the emotional issues, the use of rendered product from such sources in any animal feed raises important safety concerns. One, of course, is the transmission of disease. While the high temperatures used in the rendering process cer-

Horse meat is not commonly used in cat foods manufactured and distributed in the United States.

tainly destroy most common microbes and parasites present in the animal carcasses, some other disease processes remain unknown or unclear, although very unlikely to occur under such conditions. However, *meat and bone meal* recently came under closer scrutiny when it was suspected that "mad-cow disease" may be spread by cows eating other infected cows that had been ground up, rendered, and recycled in animal feed. In response, a ban was proposed to prohibit the practice of feeding ruminant-to-ruminant material.

Another major concern involves drug residues left in the bodies of animals that were put down or that died during medical treatment. For example, preliminary studies have shown that sodium pentobarbital, a drug commonly used to euthanize small animals, does not break down completely during the rendering process. Exactly how much of this residue, if any, survives and winds up in animal feed is not known. Until recently, available testing procedures could not readily detect such residues in pet foods or pet food ingredients and therefore could not be used reliably to monitor products on the market. But according to the FDA-CVM, preliminary reports on a new testing method show reliable and promising results as a tool for detecting drug residues.

Chapter 4

Understanding Cat Food Labels

Choosing a Cat Food

With so many brands, varieties, and flavors to choose from, it's relatively easy to find a good-quality cat food that your cat enjoys and that is convenient for you to serve. By being familiar with the labeling terms on cat foods, and by understanding your cat's specific health and life cycle needs, you will be able to make better choices. This requires working closely with your veterinarian, taking your cat in for regular checkups and routine health exams, and asking questions about the foods you're feeding. When selecting a cat food, first ask your veterinarian or breeder to recommend a favorite brand. In addition, follow these general guidelines:

• Look for the words *complete and balanced*, as substantiated by AAFCO protocols, on the label. If the statement is not there, the food is probably a snack or a treat and is not appropriate for daily rations.

• Select only those brands that have substantiated their claims of complete and balanced nutrition through animal feeding trials. This, too, will be stated on the label.

• Choose a formula that is appropriate for your cat's current life stage. For example, growing kittens need a kitten chow, a feline

Young, active cats need a more "energy-dense," higher-protein-content food than sedate, nonbreeding adults.

growth and reproduction formula, or a food that meets the nutritional needs of "all life stages" of cats. Nonbreeding adults can be fed foods formulated for all life stages or for "adult maintenance," depending on their individual needs. However, an adult maintenance formula is *not* an appropriate choice for a growing kitten or a pregnant or nursing queen.

• Read the first five ingredients on the label. At least one animal protein source, such as poultry meal, meat, or a meat byproduct, should be high on the list. Its appearance far down on the list indicates that the food's protein content has been boosted by plant protein sources.

• Call the toll-free telephone number provided on the package and ask questions about product content, digestibility, and research.

Judge for yourself whether the representatives seem knowledgeable and forthcoming with their answers.

• Consider the manufacturer's experience and commitment to animal health and nutrition. After all, a manufacturer's reputation is perhaps the best assurance that correct practices and quality standards are observed and met during pet food processing.

Remember, too, that product quality has nothing to do with the amount of advertising exposure the product receives. Price is not always a reliable indicator of quality either. The best indicator of a food's quality is how well your cat maintains its weight and overall body and coat condition on a particular dietary regimen. For example, skin problems and a poor hair coat may indicate that something is lacking in the diet, warranting further investigation. To provide your cat with variety and appetite appeal, pick at least two or three high-quality products your cat seems to like and use them interchangeably.

Deciphering a Cat Food Label

Pet food companies are required by law to supply certain nutritional information on their labels. The label must state whether the product provides complete and balanced nutrition and whether it's adequate for all life stages or for just certain life stages of cats. In addition, the words *cat food*, or a similar description, must appear conspicuously on the label to distinguish the product from dog food or any other type of food. No part of the label can contain false information or make misleading comparisons to other cat foods, and pictures on the label cannot misrepresent the contents. Label components include:

Product and Brand Name

The product name, which describes the contents, must appear on the principal display panel. This is the part of the label displayed prominently and seen under normal retail sale conditions. Although not required by law, the brand name, which identifies the pet food company, usually also appears on the principal display panel, too, and is often a part of the product name. If the product name includes a flavor designation, such as *beef flavored cat food*, the words *beef* and *flavored* must be displayed in the same size and color of type. In addition, the source of the beef flavor, which may be beef, beef digest, beef and bone meal, or some similar ingredient, must be disclosed in the ingredients listing. If the product is called *tuna cat food*, then tuna must constitute 95 percent of the total weight of all ingredients, except added water, in the food and at least 70 percent of the total product formula, including

added water. Similarly, if the product is called *tuna dinner*, *tuna platter, tuna supper*, or some similar designation, tuna must comprise at least 25 percent but less than 95 percent of the total weight of all ingredients, except added water, and at least 10 percent of the total product formula. If the product simply says *with tuna*, then the tuna content can be much less, as little as 3 percent. Obviously, if a product contains more than one ingredient, it cannot be designated as *100% beef* or *all beef*, as this would be untrue. Labeling terms and ingredients are defined in AAFCO's Pet Food Regulations in its *Official Publication*. (Please refer to Useful Addresses and Literature in the back of this book.)

Net Weight/Quantity

The declaration of net weight required on the principal display

Although cats evolved to be natural, efficient predators, meat comprises only a portion of their total diet.

A cat food label has two main parts, the principal display panel and the information panel, which share important details about product use and contents.

panel allows consumers to compare prices of products based on weight. Weights appear in the lower third of the display panel and are usually given in both American standard measures (ounces and pounds) and metric measures (grams or kilograms).

Ingredients List

On a label's information panel, ingredients are supposed to be listed in descending order of predominance by weight, but in some cases this may be misleading. For example, meat may be listed first, leading the consumer to believe the product contains mostly meat, when in reality the summation of separately listed grains and cereals makes plant material the predominant ingredient.

A good way to check specific ingredients and their amounts is simply to call the manufacturer's number on the package and ask for the data. Many of the larger companies have consulting veterinarians

and/or nutritionists willing to answer consumer questions. If a manufacturer seems unwilling or unprepared to share the information, it may mean the substantiating research is either nonexistent or unfavorable.

If AAFCO has established a name and definition for a particular ingredient, that name must be used on labels. If an ingredient has no AAFCO-established name, it must be listed by its common name. The ingredients list can contain no reference to quality or grade, and all ingredients must be shown in letters of the same type size and color.

Nutritional Adequacy Statement

To prove their products meet AAFCO's nutritional guidelines, cat food manufacturers can choose one of two methods to substantiate their claim of complete and balanced nutrition:

- they can formulate the food to meet an established nutrient profile, which can be achieved by calculation, or
- they can test the food by feeding it to cats.

Feeding trials are the most expensive and time-consuming method. But they offer greater assurance that the formula is adequately nutritious, because the product has been test-fed to cats for a specified period of time according to AAFCO protocols. Any product that has undergone feeding trials usually says so on the package. Look for the company's statement of nutritional adequacy, which, if test-fed to animals, should say something similar to "Animal feeding tests using AAFCO procedures substantiate that [this brand name] provides complete and balanced nutrition for the maintenance of adult cats." A product that has been substantiated simply by adhering to formulation will make no mention of feeding trials on the label and instead might state something like "[Product name] is formulated to meet the nutritional levels established by the AAFCO Cat Food Nutrient Profiles for all life stages."

Except for exempt snacks and treats, foods that are not complete and balanced must be distinguished from foods designed for daily rations with the words *for intermittent feeding only* or *not to be fed as a sole diet* on the label. If the food is a therapeutic diet that is designed to be used only under the supervision of a veterinarian, the label must say so, as in "Use only as directed by your veterinarian," along with any other appropriate AAFCO labeling statements.

Guaranteed Analysis

The required "guaranteed analysis," listing content percentages of certain nutrients, must state on the label's information panel whether minimum or maximum amounts were met, but doesn't have to list actual concentrations of specific

100% – 78% = 22%

$$\frac{10\%}{22\%} = 45\%$$

78% Moisture

10% Protein

Other dry matter

Guaranteed analysis

45% Protein

55% Other dry matter

Dry weight analysis

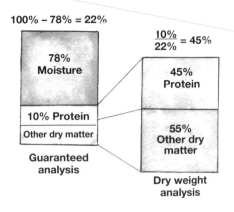

Having determined the dry matter content of a food, you may calculate a dry weight analysis for each ingredient. For example, a canned food shows label guarantees of 10 percent protein and 78 percent water. By dry weight analysis, however, the protein is 10 percent divided by 22 percent (dry matter), which equals 45 percent protein.

nutrients. While these percentages are fairly close to the real amounts in many cases (except, perhaps, when it comes to the amount of fat in canned foods), the problem with not knowing how much a product exceeds the minimum requirement for a certain nutrient, such as protein, is that sometimes too much can be just as bad as too little, depending on a cat's age and condition. What this means is that, while foods formulated for all life stages of cats are designed to meet normal nutritional needs from kittenhood through seniorhood, some individuals, particularly those predisposed to certain health problems, may get far more of certain nutrients than they need.

According to AAFCO's regulation, the information required in the guaranteed analysis must appear in the following format:

- crude protein (minimum percentage)
- crude fat (minimum percentage)
- crude fiber (maximum percentage)
- moisture (maximum percentage)

The word *crude* refers to total content as determined by laboratory trial. The term should not be confused with any guarantee of quality or digestibility of the protein, fat, or fiber.

Dry Weight Analysis

Because label percentages are based on the entire food formula, water and all, one must use a standard basis of comparison when reading labels of different types of cat foods. One way to accomplish this is to calculate the product's dry weight, or the food content that would be left if all of the water were removed. First, determine the percentages of moisture and dry matter in the food. The guaranteed analysis already contains part of this information. If the label says the moisture content is 78 percent, subtract that figure from 100 percent (total food formula) to calculate the dry matter. In this example, the dry matter in the food is 22 percent.

Once you've calculated the dry matter, you can do a dry weight analysis for each nutrient in the food, based on the label guarantees. The formula for this is simple:

$$\frac{\% \text{ nutrient}}{\% \text{ dry matter}}$$

For example, we've already determined that the dry matter is 22 percent, now we want to know how much of that matter is protein. The guaranteed analysis on the label says the food contains a minimum of 10 percent crude protein. That 10-percent figure is based on the food's total formula, including moisture content. However, on a dry matter basis, the protein content is:

$$\frac{10\% \text{ protein}}{22\% \text{ dry matter}} = 45\%$$

To support normal growth and reproduction, AAFCO recommends that at least 30 percent of a cat's diet be protein. For maintenance of adult cats, protein content should be at least 26 percent. Remember, these are recommended *minimum* amounts, based on dry matter, that foods should contain. In the above example, the label guarantees the product to be no less than 45 percent protein (dry weight basis), but it doesn't tell you whether the

actual protein content exceeds that stated minimum. Although the actual amount is likely to be relatively close to that minimum, within say 46 percent to 48 percent, knowing the exact amount might be important if, for example, your cat requires a protein-reduced diet because of a medical condition.

The point is that, although the dry weight analysis is a good way to compare nutrient percentages in different types of foods, it's not an exact measurement of daily nutrient intake. Remember, label guarantees are expressed either in minimum (not less than) or maximum (not more than) percentages, but not in actual amounts. If you're concerned about feeding too much or too little of a certain nutrient, consult your veterinarian. He or she can best assess your cat's body condition and individual nutritional needs.

Manufacturer Information

The label has to provide the name and address of the pet food manufacturer, packer, or distributor. Most manufacturers also list a toll-free telephone number, which is useful when a consumer has questions or complaints about the product or its contents.

Feeding Instructions

Complete and balanced rations must provide guidelines for feeding a daily amount per unit of body weight. The information has to be expressed in common terms. For example, most dry food labels use the recognizable household unit

To avoid overfeeding, use a standard measuring cup to mete out the amount of dry food your cat needs each day, as recommended on the product label.

of measurement, the standard 8-ounce measuring cup.

Feeding guidelines are useful but not absolute and should be used simply as a general rule or as a starting point when switching a cat to a new diet. The recommended amounts are estimates based on feeding trials and, to cover a wider variation of cats, manufacturers tend to overstate their feeding guidelines. If your cat appears to gain or lose weight on the new food, adjust the rations accordingly. Remember that actual feeding amounts vary with a cat's age, breed, size, temperament, activity, climate, and individual body metabolism.

How Much and When to Feed

There are two basic ways to feed a cat. You can offer the day's ration

or three daily meals. This method is recommended for canned foods, because they will spoil if left out too long. Removing any uneaten portion after the cat appears finished and walks away from its dish prevents spoilage and helps establish a mealtime pattern with this method.

Many owners opt for a combination of the two feeding methods. For example, some may offer a controlled canned food serving at the morning meal but leave out dry food for the remainder of the day's rations. Others elect to divide the daily rations of dry or semimoist foods into several smaller servings and leave out the portions for between-meal snacking. Regardless of the feeding method or type of food you choose, provide a bowl of fresh, clean water for your cat to drink freely at all times.

Product Feeding Guidelines

As a guide to how much to feed, follow the feeding instructions on the cat food package as a start. Then, as you observe your cat's eating habits, gradually add or subtract food as needed. Remember, recommended feeding amounts vary widely among brands and types of cat foods. Because feeding guidelines vary significantly from one food to another, check labels each time you switch brands to make sure you're not grossly overfeeding or underfeeding the recommended amount for a particular product. It's also a good idea

either free-choice or in controlled servings. With free-choice feeding, you put out the measured daily ration and allow your cat to eat at will. This method is recommended only with dry or semimoist diets. When feeding controlled servings, you divide the day's ration into two

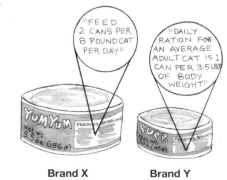

Brand X **Brand Y**

to weigh your cat so you know how much cat you've got to feed.

For example, an energy-dense premium dry food may recommend ⅓ to ½ cup (using a standard, 8-ounce measuring cup) of food daily for a cat that weighs five to 10 pounds and ½ to ⅔ cup for a cat weighing 10 to 15 pounds. Another dry brand may be less specific about how much the cat weighs and simply recommend feeding one full 8-ounce measuring cup of food per day. That's a big difference!

Because canned foods come in different sizes, some simple arithmetic may occasionally be required to figure out the proper amount to feed your cat. For example, one 5.5-ounce canned variety may recommend one can per 6.5 pounds of body weight, while another 3-ounce brand may set the daily ration at one can per 3.5 pounds of body weight. In the latter case, if your cat weighs 7 pounds, it would need two cans per day to receive the recommended daily allowance of nutrients in that particular food, and three cans if the cat weighs 10.5 pounds.

Because some foods, particularly the high-quality premium brands, are designed to be more digestible and more energy dense than others, they require less amount per pound of body weight to supply adequate nutrition. This means you can feed a smaller amount, and the feeding guidelines on a premium cat food are usually quite specific.

Avoid Overfeeding

Although many cat owners prefer the convenience of free-choice feeding, leaving out too much food for a cat to nibble on throughout the day can result in a fat cat. While some cats will eat just enough to satisfy their caloric requirements, others will overeat when given the opportunity. For cats that are overweight or on special diets, the controlled serving feeding method may be more appropriate. (Refer also to the chapter on "Obesity: Making Fat Cats Fit," page 86.)

When feeding free-choice, however, it's especially important to measure and leave out only the recommended daily ration for each 24-hour period, as opposed to filling a huge bowl or a bulk feeder with several days' worth of food. Self-feeders that dispense food from a bulk hopper as the cat eats are handy for when you go away on an occasional overnight trip and need to leave out extra food for your cat. But for routine feedings,

Overfeeding can lead to overeating, which often results in a tubby tabby. As in humans, obesity in cats carries serious health risks.

it's better to leave out only one day's ration at a time.

At one time, it was thought that nibbling on dry foods throughout the day predisposed cats to feline urologic syndrome (FUS) by allowing the urine pH to become too alkaline. But this is no longer the case. Today, most major cat food brands have been reformulated with acidifying ingredients to better maintain urine pH levels within normal acidic ranges (see page 16). In most cases, free-choice feeding is the recommended method for offering dry foods. Cats also seem to prefer this method. While dogs tend to gorge on their food and gulp an entire meal at once, cats are natural snack feeders. When allowed to feed free-choice, they will eat 10 or more small meals during a 24-hour period. Perhaps this routine approximates how they would catch small prey in the wild.

Feeding in a Multicat Household

Mealtime in a multicat household can be quite a hectic affair, espe-

In a multicat household, competitive eating can inspire some felines to overeat, while others may not get enough. The best strategy is to feed cats in separate bowls, and, if necessary, in separate locations.

cially if one or more cats require a special diet. Free-choice feeding can inspire competitive eating so that some cats may overeat while others may not get enough. If this happens in your household, switching to supervised mealtimes may be the better solution. If this isn't practical for you, try feeding the problem eaters in a separate room. If one cat is on a special or therapeutic diet, you will have to feed it in a separate location as well. Plus, you will have to restrict its access to the normal cats' food.

Remember, the amount of food your cats require each day varies with their age, weight, environment, and activity level. Most adult cats thrive on two meals a day, morning and evening. Others do just as well on canned food portions for breakfast, combined with dry rations left out for free-choice nibbling throughout the day. Whatever routine you prefer, feed your cats at the same time and in the same place each day. Provide each cat with its own bowl, and space the bowls far enough apart to allow adequate feeding zones in between. Also, be diligent about keeping the food bowls clean. Adjust the rations and feeding schedule as necessary to maintain optimum body weight and condition. Because a veterinarian can best assess an animal's condition, be sure to discuss your feeding program when you take your cats in for annual checkups.

Chapter 5
Life-Cycle Nutrition

The Life-Cycle Concept

Good nutrition depends a great deal on a cat's age, activity level, and state of health. What's good for a kitten is not necessarily the best choice for a sedentary, middle-aged cat, and vice versa. In fact, research has shown that certain nutrients consumed at too high or too low levels during early life stages may contribute to health problems later in life. This knowledge ended the old "womb-to-tomb" practice of feeding cats one food their entire lives and ushered in a new era of life-cycle nutrition. Today, life-cycle formulas scientifically tailored to meet a cat's nutritional needs during different stages of its life compete for grocery store shelf space.

The AAFCO Nutrient Profiles for Cat Foods include adult maintenance and growth and reproduction formulas. Adult maintenance formulas are intended to provide complete and balanced nutrition for nonbreeding male and female cats age one year and older. Growth and repro-duction formulas are designed for kittens up to one year old and for breeding females that are pregnant or lactating. The two basic AAFCO profiles vary in the specific amounts of protein, amino acids, vitamins, and minerals that must be present in the food to be considered complete and balanced for these different life stages. For example, to support normal growth and reproduction, foods designed for kittens and breeding queens must contain higher amounts of protein and cer-tain other nutrients than those intended primarily for the mainte-nance of nonbreeding adult cats.

In a nutshell, life-cycle nutrition means that a kitten's nutritional needs will change over time as it grows and matures into adulthood and old age.

Whatever profile the food meets, manufacturers must validate their nutritional and life stage claims in one of two ways: by testing the cat food in live feeding trials or by demonstrating through calculation or laboratory analysis that the nutrient levels in the formula meet AAFCO requirements. The package label discloses the method used (see page 58). For a food to bear the claim of "nutritionally complete and balanced for *all life stages*," it must pass all growth and reproduction tests, as outlined in the AAFCO protocols. Foods that satisfy these test protocols are considered suitable for cats of all ages, from kittens to senior citizens. An adult maintenance formula, however, must meet only the maintenance test requirements; it does *not* have to pass growth and reproduction testing. This is because maintenance formulas are intended primarily for nonbreeding adults that

If your grown cat stays indoors and is a sedate "couch potato," an "adult maintenance" formula cat food may be a suitable choice.

don't need the extra protein and energy that growing or breeding animals demand. Therefore, a food labeled as "nutritionally complete and balanced for *adult* cats" or "for the maintenance of adult cats" is *not* an adequate diet for growing kittens or pregnant or nursing queens and should not be fed to animals in these life stages.

Selecting a Life-Cycle Formula

When choosing any cat food, the important thing to remember is that no *one* perfect pet food exists for every cat and for every owner. Although pet food labels provide helpful information, choosing a cat food solely by label contents or by brand name is unwise. Instead, base your selection on how well your cat performs and maintains its overall condition on a particular food. Start with high-quality commercial products your breeder or veterinarian recommends. Select foods formulated to meet the nutritional requirements of your cat's current stage of life, whether it's a kitten, a pregnant or lactating queen, a nonbreeding adult, or a senior citizen. For example, if your adult cat is active, goes outside, or gets plenty of exercise, choose a food formulated for all life stages to ensure that it receives enough energy to meet its needs. However, if you have a middle-aged "couch potato," an adult maintenance formula might be a suitable choice. Keep in mind that your cat's nutritional needs change as it ages. Some cats that develop kidney disease or other medical problems may need to switch to a special diet available through veterinarians. So, during annual checkups, as your veterinarian assesses your cat's condition, be sure to ask about your pet's changing dietary needs as it grows and matures, and make adjustments as necessary.

To avoid causing digestive upsets, always make recommended changes to your cat's diet gradually, over a period of at least a week. Begin by mixing small amounts of the new food with the current rations. Gradually increase the amount of new food as you decrease the amount of old food until the changeover is complete.

Feeding Kittens

For their first full year, kittens should receive a high-quality commercial cat food formulated for feline growth. At least 30 to 40 percent of the kittens' diet should be protein to meet the extra demands of their active, rapidly growing bodies. Cat foods guaranteed to be complete and balanced for *all life stages* of the cat are suitable for kittens, but, as previously discussed, adult maintenance formulas are not. Diets for adult cats are generally designed to offer less protein and energy than kittens need to sustain normal, healthy growth. So, when selecting a food for your kitten,

Growth and reproduction formulas are designed for the special nutritional needs of growing kittens as well as pregnant or nursing queens. For proper growth and strong bones, feed a good-quality kitten kibble for a kitten's first full year.

make sure the product is labeled either for "growth and reproduction" or for "all life stages" of the cat.

Aside from being made to meet the specific protein and energy requirements of growing kittens, dry kitten kibble is also patterned into smaller pellets that make it easier for tiny kitten mouths to chew and swallow. For the first several weeks of life, mother's milk supplies all the nutrients and calories growing kittens need. (For information about hand-fostering orphaned kittens, see page 124.) The queen will suckle them for six or seven weeks, but usually by four weeks of age kittens can begin experimenting with small amounts of soft, solid foods.

Weaning

To avoid upsetting the kittens' digestive systems, make the change to solid food gradually over a one- or two-week period. By

During the first few weeks of life, mother's milk provides all the nutrients kittens need. Once weaned, however, kittens will benefit from a high-quality growth and reproduction formula for their first full year.

about six or eight weeks, they should, in most cases, be fully weaned and ready to leave their mother, although many breeders of purebred cats will not release their kittens to new homes until 12 to 16 weeks of age. The reason for this practice is twofold: Certain breeds mature more slowly than others; plus, some breeders prefer that their kittens have a complete set of vaccinations before letting them go to a strange, new environment.

To begin weaning, offer a commercial kitten milk replacer, such as KMR (available through veterinarians and pet stores). If this is not readily available, you may temporarily resort to a half-and-half mixture of warm water and evaporated milk in a shallow bowl or saucer. (Avoid using homogenized cow's milk, as this can cause diarrhea.) Starting with a saucer of warm milk introduces the kittens to the idea of eating a familiar food out of a dish. However, don't expect their table manners to be polished and pristine the first time. They will almost cer-

tainly climb in with all four feet, so be prepared to mimic mama cat's rough tongue by gently wiping them clean with a warm, damp washcloth afterwards. As the kittens become accustomed to eating out of a dish, start adding small amounts of canned kitten food or meat varieties of human baby food to this milk formula. If you use human baby food, experts recommend avoiding varieties that contain onion or onion powder. Studies suggest that onions contain a compound that, if fed in large enough amounts over a period of time, may damage red blood cells and cause anemia in cats. Most important, human baby food does *not* contain all of the nutrients growing kittens need. For this reason, it should be used sparingly and only on a short-term basis, as you transition from mother's milk or milk formula to solid cat food during a period of about a week or two. Fed on a habitual, long-term basis, human baby food alone cannot supply adequate nutrition for kittens and cats.

As you gradually increase the amount of solid food, gradually decrease the milk formula until the changeover is complete. As you begin decreasing the milk formula, remember to place clean, fresh water in a shallow bowl for the kittens to drink. Also, once the kittens become accustomed to eating moist, solid foods, it's time to start mixing in some dry kitten food. At first, soften the dry food with warm water or milk formula to make it easier to chew. Taste preferences are established at an early age, so if you want your kitten to like eating dry food when it grows up, it's important to start getting it accustomed to the tastes and textures while it's young. By the time kittens are old enough to be fully weaned, they should be able to chew dry food.

How Much to Feed

Because they have smaller stomachs, kittens need to be fed in smaller quantities than adult cats, but their higher energy demands require more frequent feedings to sustain normal growth. Newly weaned kittens will need three or four small meals a day, or leave out dry food for them to eat free-choice. At six months, reduce the number of feedings to two a day. By this age, kittens are almost fully grown but are still quite active and playful. Because their energy demands remain high, continue feeding an appropriate kitten food for another six months. To determine the proper amount to feed, follow the general feeding recommendations on the pet food package, but be prepared to adjust the amount, as necessary, to meet each individual kitten's needs. During their vital growth and development stage, it's a good idea to offer kittens as much food as they want to eat. Unlike puppies, kittens are not gorge feeders and usually do a good job of self-regulating the amount they eat according to how much energy they burn.

Feeding Pregnant and Lactating Queens

To aid in fetal development and milk production, breeding female cats, called *queens,* need two to four times more food than they normally eat to adequately provide for their growing kittens. To accommodate this extra need, feed a high-quality, energy-dense growth and feline reproduction formula throughout gestation and lactation. Offer the queen her meals free-choice or on demand, as much as she will eat. Even with abundant food available, she likely will self-regulate her food consumption according to how much energy she requires for herself and her kittens.

Some breeders believe that queens need calcium supplements during lactation to prevent a condition called *eclampsia,* or milk fever. This potentially fatal condition occurs

Milk, while okay for kittens during their transition to solid food, is not a suitable diet for adult cats. Like humans, many grown cats develop a lactose intolerance to milk and will experience diarrhea if they drink it.

when the queen's system is depleted of the essential nutrient, calcium. However, unless advised by a veterinarian, regular supplementation is neither necessary nor recommended when feeding a complete and balanced cat food formulated specifically for reproduction. Diets formulated for this life stage contain enough calcium to meet the extra needs during pregnancy and lactation.

Throughout her pregnancy, the female should show a steady increase in weight as well as a gradual increase in food intake. As the time of birth nears, hormonal changes may make her lose her appetite temporarily, but usually this is no cause for worry, unless it becomes prolonged and the queen starts to lose condition. If the queen starts to look thin, or if her fur becomes brittle and coarse, ask your veterinarian to evaluate her and your feeding program.

Feeding Adult Cats

Sedate or moderately active adult cats not used for breeding need enough nutrients, fiber, and protein to satisfy their appetites, yet fewer calories to prevent them from getting fat. For such cats, a combination of canned and dry foods formulated for *adult maintenance* is generally a good choice. But active, athletic cats, especially ones allowed outdoors, or an intact tom used for breeding, may thrive better on foods formulated for *all life stages*, because, as previously discussed, these formulas meet extra energy requirements. The appropriate selection depends on whether your cat will eat the food and on whether it maintains good body condition while on the food.

One common feeding mistake many owners make in feeding their adult cats is leaving out indiscriminately large amounts of dry food to nibble on at will. While many cats can self-regulate their food consumption according to how much energy they burn, others cannot. Although they are not gorge feeders like dogs, some cats will overeat and grow fat, given ample opportunity and an overabundant food supply. The key to successful free-choice feeding is to carefully measure and leave out only enough food to meet the animal's recommended rations per day or per meal, then replenish the bowl at the next mealtime interval. Problems commonly arise in multicat households, however, where competitive eating may induce some cats to overeat and gain weight.

Indeed, obesity has become such a prevalent problem among pets in North America (see also Chapter 7, Obesity, beginning on page 86) that some press reports have advised people against feeding their cats free-choice. Unfortunately, this has led to a great deal of confusion and debate over the best way to feed cats. The answer is, *there is no universally best way*. The best way is simply what works best for both you and your cat. For example, some cats do well on two or three meals a day. During each meal, a controlled portion is set out in a bowl for 30 minutes or so, then removed, regardless of whether all of the food is consumed. Other cats will lose condition if fed this way, because they are snack-eaters by nature, preferring to nibble and consume several small meals during a 24-hour period. These snack-eaters often don't consume enough food at two or three designated mealtimes to fully meet the day's nutritional allowance. For cats that seem to prefer snack-feeding, it is

If your dog tends to steal food from your cat's bowl, feed the cat in a higher place where the dog can't reach.

better to measure out the daily ration in a bowl and leave it for free-choice nibbling throughout the day. But avoid leaving out an overabundant supply of food that could last for days.

Much depends on what the cat has become accustomed to since kittenhood, but the type of food can also be an important determining factor in how you feed your cat. For example, canned foods spoil if left out all day, so offering controlled portions at set mealtimes is the best way to provide this type of food (see page 61). Dry and semi-moist foods, on the other hand, can be left out for free-choice feeding without spoiling. In addition, free-choice feeding is often recommended on dry kibble package labels because of the balancing influence of acidifying ingredients on the urine pH (see page 114).

Feeding Older Cats

Generally speaking, a cat becomes a senior citizen when it reaches the 10-year mark. Although some purebreds tend to age faster and live fewer years than mixed breeds, the average life expectancy of the cat is 14 or 15 years. With today's better nutrition and veterinary care, some cats are even living to be 20 and older! As with many people, a cat's rate of metabolism gradually slows with age, and individuals typically grow less active. If arthritis develops in the joints, this, too, will cause the activity level to decline. Elderly cats also become less resistant to disease and infection, and their organs become less efficient at digesting food or clearing waste products from the body. These physical changes may require some important adjustments to the cat's daily diet to ensure continued good health.

Because their energy needs decline with less activity, some middle-aged and senior cats may require fewer calories to avoid becoming obese. Those that tend to get fat may thrive on a high-fiber, reduced-calorie "light" or "senior" formula. At your cat's annual checkup, ask your veterinarian to dispense or recommend one. The higher fiber content is designed to satisfy the cat's appetite so that it doesn't feel hungry, even though it is consuming fewer calories, less fat, and slightly less protein.

Not all cats have a weight problem when they get older. In fact, more cats are fat at middle-age—starting at 5 or 6 years old—than they are at an advanced age. Research at the Waltham Centre has shown that digestibility, or the ability to efficiently extract and utilize nutrients in food, tends to decline with age. Many older cats have to eat more to get enough energy, because they don't digest their food as well as they used to. This explains why some begin to lose weight and get thin in their later years, after age 11 or so, even though they check out as basically healthy with no diabetes, no kidney disease, and so on. Because their organs can no longer handle food as efficiently as when they were younger, they simply cannot get the same nutrient value from the same food.

The best judge of how well your cat is maintaining its body condition on a particular diet is your veterinarian. If you think your cat may be too fat or too thin, mention your concerns at your next visit.

What's an owner to do? If a senior cat starts to grow thin, but otherwise checks out healthy at the veterinarian's office and has no signs of kidney disease or other medical problems, consider switching to an energy-dense food formulated to provide optimum digestibility. Ask your veterinarian to recommend a suitable brand. Often, a good-quality kitten chow or feline growth and reproduction formula may do the job. This recommendation contradicts what some owners may have heard or read about always selecting lower protein foods to ease the burden on an older cat's kidneys. To clarify this misconception, there is no definitive proof that the higher protein content of certain foods *causes* renal problems. It is true, however, that once a cat has exhibited signs of renal dysfunction, it definitely requires a lower-protein therapeutic diet to manage the condition and to avoid further compromising the kidneys' ability to process body waste products. Certain other medical conditions may require special diets as well. Your veterinarian can best evaluate your cat's needs in this regard.

If an older cat is otherwise healthy, a higher-protein food, such as one formulated for kittens or for all life stages, is not necessarily detrimental. Nevertheless, before switching to a richer, energy-dense food, it's a good idea to have the cat checked by a veterinarian first to determine its health status and to rule out any underlying health problems. Sometimes, kidney problems don't even become readily apparent until well over half of the normal renal function is lost. Symptoms of kidney dysfunction include increased thirst, increased urination, weight loss, and intermittent vomiting (see page 117).

As with cats of all ages, a sudden loss of appetite in the elderly cat may be a sign that the animal is sick or in pain. Often, an older cat may refuse to eat if it has developed dental disease. Sore gums and aching teeth may simply make eating too painful. Even more serious is the possibility that bacteria from inflamed gums (gingivitis) may leak into the bloodstream and damage other organs. To avoid such problems, have your cat's condition assessed regularly by a veterinarian. (See pages 126-128 for more information on dental care.)

Chapter 6
Basic Mealtime DOs and DON'Ts

DO Discourage Finicky Behavior

Most cats really are not the finicky eaters that advertisers would have us believe. Cats are, however, creatures of habit that flourish on routine, particularly when it comes to food. Many develop taste preferences early in life, at a crucial developmental stage when they are apparently learning to recognize what's edible and what's not. Once learned, taste preferences can be difficult to change, even if the cat's health

Few cats will eat cold canned food straight out of the refrigerator. Before serving, warm it a few seconds in the microwave, then test with your finger to make sure it's not too hot.

depends upon it. Some cats simply seem to get addicted to one food and will refuse to eat anything else. It follows logically, therefore, that the way to avoid creating finicky behavior is to feed cats a variety of foods, in form, texture, and flavor, right from the start.

DO Offer Variety

To alternate form, for example, many owners prefer to feed canned food for the morning meal and leave out enough dry food to cover the remainder of the daily rationed amount. Whether you allow your cat to self-feed or provide it with single-serving meals, select at least two or three types and varieties of food that your cat seems to enjoy and rotate these regularly. Introduce new flavors on occasion. Accustom your cat to different food shapes and textures, too. Store selections abound with everything from crunchy nuggets to round pellets to bite-size fish shapes. The artificial coloring added to some foods is meaningless to cats and obviously intended only to make the products look more pleasing to the human consumer. The different shapes and textures, however, apparently do matter to cats, because much product research centers on designing a food with just the right "mouth feel" that will please and entice the animal to eat.

Avoid feeding only canned or semimoist foods, because cats fed soft diets exclusively may be more prone to dental problems than those receiving dry rations. Also, cats inclined toward finicky eating behavior are more likely to develop an affinity for canned foods, because the higher protein and fat content make most of these foods more palatable. Understandably, cats, like people, prefer to eat what tastes good to them, regardless of whether the food is a good choice nutritionally. But the owner who suddenly switches his cat from a steady gourmet diet to different entrees may find himself confronted with a spoiled feline that stubbornly holds out for the tastier stuff it has grown accustomed to eating.

Because forcing sudden dietary changes on a cat can result in the feline equivalent of a hunger strike, a better tactic is to make changes gradually. If your cat resists experimenting with new food forms or flavors, simply sprinkle a few kernels of dry food over its regular canned food. Over the next week or two, gradually increase the amount of new food mixed with decreasing amounts of regular food until the changeover is complete and the cat is eating its new food without a fuss.

DO Avoid Table Scraps

Feeding a cat too much "people food" also can, in some cases, contribute to finicky eating behavior, especially if the cat decides it likes your food better than its own. Furthermore, a steady fare of table scraps does not provide a balanced diet for cats. Feline nutritional requirements differ vastly from human requirements, so what's good for people is not necessarily good or better for cats. In fact, overindulging in table scraps can be downright harmful if your cat fills up too often on people food and fails to eat enough complete and balanced cat food to satisfy its daily requirements for protein, taurine, B-complex vitamins, calcium, and so on. Of course, table scraps are not all bad. It's OK to offer them in moderation, as *occasional* treats. Just don't overdo it, and avoid turning the treat offerings into a daily ritual. Experts recommend that, when offered, table scraps should comprise less than 10 percent of your cat's daily ration. Also, *never* feed your cat leftovers that you suspect might be unfit for human consumption. In all cases, garbage is garbage.

DO Avoid Vitamin Supplements

Responsible cat food manufacturers go to a lot of trouble and expense to back claims that their

It is generally OK to leave out dry food for your cat to nibble on throughout the day. But to avoid overfeeding, measure out the recommended daily ration, as indicated in the product's feeding guidelines, and leave that amount in the bowl each day.

products are nutritionally "complete and balanced" for the stated life cycle. For the most part, you can rely on a brand-name manufacturer's long-standing reputation that these claims are not grossly overstated. And generally speaking, dietary excesses pose more of a problem in many cases than do dietary deficiencies. Therefore, when feeding your cat proper amounts of high-quality commercial cat foods, vitamin and mineral supplements are unnecessary, unless recommended by a veterinarian for treatment of a specific deficiency. In fact, oversupplementing a cat's diet can cause serious health problems, whether you use natural ingredients or over-the-counter drugs. Too much of a good thing can be just as harmful as too little. For example, a diet too lavish in organ meats, particularly liver, a rich source of vitamin A, can cause an excessive buildup of vitamin A, called *hypervitaminosis,* in the body tissues. Untreated over a period of time, this condition can result in

painful and crippling skeletal changes. Of course, an occasional meal of liver or other organ meats, thoroughly cooked, but *never* raw, is OK; just don't overdo it.

Certain minerals, such as calcium and phosphorus must work together in certain proportions (see page 18) to maintain strong teeth and bones. Oversupplementing one or the other can throw this delicate balance seriously out of kilter and result in impaired metabolic processes. Some people mistakenly assume that kittens need calcium supplements to grow strong bones and teeth; however, a good-quality commercial kitten chow or growth formula cat food contains all the extra protein and minerals a growing kitten needs. The same is true for a pregnant and nursing queen. As long as you're feeding her a high-quality cat food designed for feline reproduction, no supplements should be required, unless your veterinarian specifically recommends it.

Vitamin D must be present in adequate amounts for effective absorption and utilization of calcium and phosphorus, but an oversupply can create abnormal calcium deposits in the bones and soft tissues. Weakness, joint pain, and stiffness may indicate vitamin D toxicity. Cortisone helps relieve the pain, but once abnormal calcification has occurred, the damage to body tissues and organs is not so easily undone.

To prevent these vitamin toxicities, avoid using cod-liver oil and other fish-liver oils, which are rich sources of vitamins A and D, as daily dietary supplements. Some breeders may still recommend these substances as a way to improve the sheen of a show cat's coat. However, feeding your cat a high-quality cat food will do more for its coat and overall appearance than any arsenal of vitamin and mineral supplements. A cat with a dry, brittle, or lackluster coat should be examined by a veterinarian, who can diagnose and properly treat the specific cause. The cause of a dull coat may have nothing to do with dietary deficiencies, in which case arbitrary supplementation by the owner would be futile, potentially dangerous, and a waste of money.

Of course, some cats may require supplementation under certain circumstances. For example, the nutritional needs of a show cat may change during show season when it is subjected to the stresses of extensive travel and ring competition. Cats recovering from illness or injury may require temporary supplementation. But always in such cases, supplementation is safest when given under the advice and guidance of a veterinarian.

DO Provide Separate Feeding Bowls

Provide every cat in your household with its own feeding bowl. When two or more cats eat from the same dish, the dominant, more aggressive personality inevitably consumes the larger share of food

and nutrients. Competitive eating in this manner often contributes to obesity, because it can compel some cats to engage in overeating behaviors, downing half or all of the other cat's portion, whenever they get the chance. Besides, competitive eating is bound to be thoroughly unpleasant and unnecessarily stressful for your feline companions. So why subject them to it? Instead, offer food in separate bowls. If necessary to quell competition, feed cats in separate locations or supervise mealtimes to ensure that each cat eats out of its own dish. If one cat must be on a special diet, it will be imperative to feed it in a separate area to ensure that it doesn't creep over to a buddy's bowl and snatch a few forbidden morsels. This strategy will also help you know for sure whether the proper cat consumed the special food.

When cats and dogs live together, a dog often will develop a penchant for cat food, simply because the higher protein content of cat food makes it taste better than dog chow.

If you have more than one cat in your household, feed each separately, instead of using one communal bowl.

If your dog starts stealing food from your cat, place the cat's dish out of the dog's reach, either in a separate area or higher up, such as on a countertop. Likewise, discourage your cat from sampling too much of the dog's food, and thus spoiling its appetite for a balanced cat food meal.

DO Feed Indoors, If Possible

Feeding cats outdoors, particularly leaving out dry food, often attracts unwanted insects and wildlife—crows, opossums, and stray cats—that follow the scent of a ready-made meal. Besides being a nuisance, these creatures may transmit diseases or parasites to your cat if they eat from the same dish. Therefore, if you must feed your cat outdoors, take up the bowl immediately after it finishes eating. Do not leave food outdoors for free-choice feeding. Whether feeding inside or outside, always wash pet feeding bowls between meals.

Stainless steel or ceramic, lead-free bowls are easier to keep clean than plastic dishes, which tend to warp in hot water and harbor food odors and bacteria in tiny crevices.

DO Feed in a Quiet Location

Cats appreciate ambiance when they're eating, and they can lose their appetite quickly when too much commotion disturbs their dining. Remember how you sometimes feel after eating in a noisy, crowded fast-food restaurant? Eating in a hectic environment can affect cats the same way and cause them to suffer periods of intestinal distress or even vomit their food afterward. Bolting food down too quickly is another problem brought on by stress factors. So if, at mealtimes, your kitchen tends to resemble lunch hour at the corner grill, feed kitty in a quieter corner of the house, away from the hustle and bustle.

DO Choose Bowls Carefully

Although they're more expensive, stainless steel, ceramic, or glass feeding bowls have several advantages over plastic dishes. They can be safely sterilized in a dishwasher, whereas plastic dishes are more likely to melt or warp. Being porous, plastic dishes tend to retain odors, even after washing. Although your nose may smell nothing, an accumulation of stale odors can cause a keen-nosed feline to start turning away from perfectly good meals. Also, if scratched, plastic dishes may harbor bacteria in the tiny ridges and creases. This is especially undesirable because it can result in gastrointestinal upsets for your cat. Another problem with plastic dishes is that some cats apparently develop a sensitivity to the chemicals used in making plastic material, although there is no conclusive evidence to support this suspicion. Still, some cats have shown signs of feline acne and allergies, including itchy bald spots and crusty sores around the mouth and nose, that appeared to improve after replacing the plastic bowls with ceramic or stainless steel ones. Certainly, plenty of cat owners use plastic feeding dishes without encountering these ill effects. But it's important to be aware of potential problems so that you can readily recognize them if they arise. If you choose plastic bowls, replace them with new ones periodically to avoid possible odor and bacterial buildup. And be on the lookout for hypersensitivity signs around your cat's muzzle.

Also, when choosing plastic or any other kind of dishes, avoid the lightweight ones and instead select the weighted varieties. It's important to select dishes that are heavy enough not to slide across the floor as the cat eats. Just imagine how frustrated you would feel if you tried to eat out of dishes that kept sliding across the table.

Ceramic dishes are a good choice because they are heavy and solid. They also come in decorative shapes and colors, but select only those fit for human use or those labeled as lead-free. Otherwise, you have no way of knowing whether the paints and glazes used on the

Flat-faced breeds, like this Persian, usually prefer to eat from shallow, saucer-shaped bowls.

dish contain harmful lead that may leach into the food or water. Of course, glass is breakable, so select sturdy, heavy dishes that are less likely to crack or chip with daily use. Replace ceramic or glass dishes that do chip.

Many cats seem to prefer flat, shallow saucers to deep dishes, perhaps because they don't like their sensitive whiskers to rub the sides of the bowl as they eat. Some cats dislike the unpleasant sensation of their whiskers touching the bowl rim so much that they will resort to scooping the food morsels out with their paws and eating off the floor. In particular, the short-snouted, flat-faced breeds, such as the Persians, Himalayans, and Exotic Shorthairs, seem to encounter greater difficulty reaching food at the bottom of deeply scooped bowls.

Always wash feeding bowls after every meal, but, unless your cat has been ill with a contagious disease, avoid disinfecting them with bleach. Any residue could be harmful to your cat. And even if you thoroughly rinse away all residue, the odor of bleach often remains, especially in porous plastics. Even a faint, lingering odor may repel some cats from eating from that dish. Disinfection in hot water is usually sufficient, particularly if you've chosen dishwasher-safe materials.

DO Avoid Milk

Although fine for kittens, milk as a staple food for adult cats is incomplete and not a balanced diet. It should not be fed to mature cats on a daily basis, exclusive of other foods. Nor is milk a substitute for water. If your cat enjoys and tolerates milk, giving it a small amount as an occasional treat is OK; however, many adult cats develop an intolerance to milk and will experience diarrhea after drinking it. Some people suffer stomach upset and similar consequences after consuming dairy products. Called *lactose intolerance* in cats and people, this inadequate digestion of milk sugar (lactose) is caused by a deficiency of the enzyme *lactase,* which breaks down the lactose in milk. Once your cat experiences a temporary bout of loose, thin, or watery stools after lapping a saucer of warm milk, avoid offering milk, dairy products, and dairy-flavored foods thereafter. Or as an alternative, choose one of several dairy products on the market with lactase added.

DON'T Feed Meats Exclusively

Meat alone is *not* a complete and balanced meal because it lacks calcium and other important nutrients. Despite the fact that cats are carnivores, they still require a certain amount of plant and vegetable matter that, if living under natural conditions in the wild, they would normally consume from the stomachs and intestines of live prey. Commercial cat foods approximate these conditions by adding cereals and grains to complement and balance the animal protein in their formula mixes. These cereals and grains are not merely *fillers;* they provide essential nutrients that, in some cases, can be derived only from plant matter. Serious nutritional imbalances can develop as a result of feeding cats an exclusive diet of meats or fish (see page 83).

DON'T Feed Raw Meats

Besides being nutritionally incomplete, meats, if served raw or undercooked, may contain disease-causing bacteria, such as salmonellae, and parasites, such as the organism that causes toxoplasmosis. Raw organ meats especially tend to harbor roundworm larvae.

Toxoplasmosis: Toxoplasmosis is a protozoan disease that can affect humans. Cats get the disease by eating infected birds, rodents, or raw, contaminated meat. The disease can be fatal to kittens but often goes unnoticed in adult cats. When signs occur, they may include weight loss, lethargy, diarrhea, fever, pneumonia, and neurologic disturbances. Once infected, cats shed the eggs, called *oocysts,* in their feces, where they become infective in the soil one to four days later. Humans can get the disease by handling soil or litter contaminated by the feces of an infected cat, although the majority of cases in humans probably result from eating undercooked meat. Thoroughly cooking meat kills the organism and helps control the spread to humans and cats.

Of greatest concern to cat owners is the risk of birth defects when a pregnant woman becomes infected with toxoplasmosis. Tests are available to detect the disease. However, studies show that many people already possess an acquired immunity to the disease, which puts it in a much less alarming perspective. As a precaution, however, pregnant women should wear gloves while gardening or when cleaning out the cat litter box. In addition, always wash hands after performing these chores and after handling raw meat. It's also important to note that cats kept indoors and fed prepackaged pet foods have little opportunity to become infected by hunting and eating wild, contaminated prey.

Salmonella: Salmonella bacteria can cause a wide range of intestinal disorders ranging from uncompli-

cated diarrhea to life-threatening systemic illness. Although cats appear to be highly resistant to the bacteria, they can contract infection from eating contaminated raw or undercooked meats, raw eggs, and infected prey animals. Because the bacteria can spread from cat to cat owner, owners must practice strict household hygiene whenever a cat shows symptoms of illness. Affected cats shed the bacteria in their feces; therefore, litter pans should be cleaned and disinfected promptly. Again, owners should always wash hands with soap and water after handling an ill cat and after emptying litter box wastes.

DON'T Feed Dog Food

Dog foods are scientifically formulated for dogs, *not* cats. Dog chow simply does not contain enough protein, taurine, B-complex vitamins, and essential fatty acids to promote good health in cats. Depending on their age, health, and activity level, cats need at least one

Eating raw or undercooked meat is just as risky for cats as it is for people. Cats can contract parasites or infections from eating raw food, regardless of whether it's wild-caught prey or meat processed for human consumption.

and a half to two times more protein than do dogs. Cats also require the amino acid taurine in their diets, which dogs do not. Without sufficient amounts of taurine, cats can suffer degeneration of the retina, an eye disorder that can lead to blindness, and dilated cardiomyopathy, a serious heart disease that can lead to death.

DON'T Overdo the Treats

Offering kitty treats before meals is like letting your kids eat cake and ice cream before their meat and vegetables. It not only spoils the appetite, causing the cat to eat less of its regular, more nutritious food, it spoils the cat into thinking that if it holds off eating the main course long enough and begs hard enough, you'll produce the yummy goodies again. Pretty soon, you have a cat that eats mostly treats, most of which are neither formulated nor intended to serve as a complete and balanced feline diet. (People who don't believe animals can rea-

Allowing your cat to sample too much "people" food can turn it into a beggar and a finicky eater.

son well enough to behave this way have never been manipulated by a crafty cat!) Cat treats are manufactured to be highly palatable but, because they are clearly designated as snack foods, they are exempt from having to prove they are complete and balanced (although some are), and they are not required to meet the same nutritional guidelines as daily-ration cat foods. In other words, treats are generally not formulated to deliver the recommended daily amounts of vitamins, minerals, proteins, etc. Instead, they are the peanuts, potato chips, and popcorn of the cat world. And, as happens with people, cats that consume too many gourmet snacks between meals eventually turn into tubby tabbies. But treats, in moderation, certainly have their place in deepening your relationship and pleasure with your cat. They are OK on occasion, once or twice a week, but avoid offering them daily, and restrict the amount to only a few morsels at a time, *not* a whole package at one sitting.

Use the timing of treats to your advantage, too, to reward your cat for good behavior and to give a pleasant association to an otherwise unpleasant chore. For example, if you're trying to accustom your cat to grooming or toothbrushing, end its training sessions on a positive note by offering a few tasty tidbits.

DON'T Feed Chocolate

Although a favorite treat for humans, chocolate is definitely not a snack for your cat. Chocolate contains a natural stimulant, called *theobromine,* that can be, in sufficient amounts, toxic to cats and dogs. Theobromine constricts the blood vessels, diminishing the flow of the vital fluid to the brain and heart. When ingested in large amounts, the substance has been known to lead to heart attack in animals. Experts say that theobromine is more concentrated in baking chocolate squares than in regular candies and desserts, where sugar and other ingredients make up more of the recipe. Even small amounts of chocolate can cause vomiting and gastrointestinal upset when consumed by the cat who discovers a chocolate-frosted cake left exposed on the kitchen countertop. So why give your cat an opportunity to develop a liking for something potentially harmful in the first place? Keep candies, baking chocolates, frosted cakes, and other chocolate-flavored desserts covered and safely out of reach.

If you don't want your cat to become a beggar, don't offer scraps from the table. Table scraps are OK as an occasional treat, but put them in your cat's bowl.

DON'T Feed Raw Egg Whites

In addition to the risk of salmonella, raw egg whites contain a protein called *avidin* that can interfere with the body's absorption of the vitamin biotin. A water-soluble member of the B-complex, biotin aids in the synthesis of vitamin C and works in conjunction with other nutrients to keep a cat's skin and coat healthy. Signs of biotin deficiency may include dry, scaly skin, thinning fur, discharges around the nose, eyes, and mouth, small skin lesions, bloody diarrhea, and appetite and weight loss. While eggs are a good source of protein and fat for cats, they should be cooked first and *never* fed raw. In fact, a well-cooked whole egg added to the diet no more than twice a week may even improve coat sheen.

DON'T Feed Raw Fish or All-Fish Diets

Feeding cats raw fish exclusive of other foods can cause a thiamine (vitamin B1) deficiency. An enzyme called *thiaminase,* found in many kinds of raw fish, can destroy thiamine in the body and produce degenerative disease in the brain and central nervous system. Signs of thiamine deficiency include appetite loss, vomiting, seizures, and loss of coordination. An affected cat often tucks in its head and curls its body into a ball when picked up. Left untreated, the disorder is fatal.

Treatment consists of injections of thiamine or vitamin B-complex, but advanced neurologic damage is often irreversible. Fortunately, commercial cat foods contain adequate amounts of thiamine to make this condition extremely rare.

Remember, what's good for people isn't necessarily good or better for cats. Tuna is a prime example. A daily diet of canned tuna meant for human consumption can cause vitamin E deficiency in cats. Even cat foods rich in red tuna should not be fed exclusive of other flavors and varieties, no matter how fond your feline is of the taste. As the body oxidizes the high amount of unsaturated fatty acids found in tuna, fat-soluble vitamin E is destroyed. If the cat continues to receive excessive amounts of these fatty acids on an all-fish diet, *steatitis,* or yellow fat disease, may result. The resulting vitamin E deficiency becomes apparent first with flaky skin and a greasy, dull hair coat. As the disease progresses, yellow, lumpy fat deposits appear under the skin, producing an inflammatory reaction and inducing a painful response when the cat is stroked. The disease is easily prevented by avoiding an all-fish diet.

Although fish and tuna varieties of commercial cat foods generally contain adequate thiamine, vitamin E, and other supplements to guarantee complete and balanced nutrition, rotating these flavors with others containing beef, chicken, turkey, and other meats, is wise. No single brand or variety of cat food can meet *all* nutritional requirements for *all* cats *all* of the time. Different breeds in different environments may have different needs. But by offering variety, you help ensure that you're covering all nutritional bases for your cat.

DON'T Offer Alcohol

Alcohol is toxic to cats, even in small amounts, so never allow your party guests to offer your cat a little lap of spiked eggnog, beer, or martini. A cat's slight body mass cannot adequately absorb the intoxicating ingredients in alcohol, and it may quickly become tipsy. Some people think it's funny to watch a cat stagger in drunken circles; however, this practice is cruel, dangerous, and sometimes deadly. It takes only a little "hair of the dog" to affect a small animal's breathing, cause shock, and lead to death.

Tobacco can also be toxic to cats, causing drooling, shaking, twitching, and staggering. To counteract the effects of nicotine poisoning, a veterinarian must administer specific chemical injections. As one might expect, cocaine, marijuana, and similar illegal substances, particularly the inhalant varieties, are dangerous to cats. Furthermore, the deliberate or forced exposure of an animal to such substances can be construed as cruelty to animals. Signs of marijuana poisoning include behavioral changes, tremors, and convulsions. Specific medical antidotes and supportive care must be given to counteract the plant's toxins.

DON'T Feed Bones and Garbage

Garbage is garbage, so don't feed your cat spoiled food or table scraps that you would not eat. Despite the fact that cats in the wild consume the bones of their live prey, never offer your cat bones leftover from your meals. Chicken and turkey bones in particular are large and brittle enough to splinter and lodge in your cat's throat or puncture parts of the digestive tract. Keep tight lids on all trash containers so that your cat won't be tempted to forage on its own and accidentally consume inedible substances.

DON'T Let Your Cat Eat Live Prey

Although the cat evolved as a natural predator of rodents, birds, and other small prey, our modern-day city kitties lead much healthier lives and incur fewer veterinary bills if restricted from hunting and roaming freely outdoors. As previously mentioned, wild animals of prey are often infected with diseases and parasites that can be transmitted directly to your cat. Some of those unwelcome organisms, such as the protozoan that causes toxoplasmosis, can then be passed from cat to human. Cats kept indoors and fed commercial cat foods rarely encounter opportunities to become infected in this manner.

Should your cat catch a mouse in the house, however, dispose of the carcass promptly and don't allow your cat to consume it. Occa-

sionally, cats present their owners with their prey as a gift offering. Experts say this normal behavior relates to the way cats perceive their human caretakers as family members. Mother cats instinctively bring dead or stunned prey to the nest when they teach their kittens how to recognize and hunt prey. So perhaps, when bringing their prey to us, our companion cats, well aware that they are the superior hunters, are instinctively trying to teach us how to hunt better. Whatever the real motivation, never punish your cat for behaving naturally, like a cat. Simply praise your pet for its generosity, then dispose of the "gift" quickly so that your feline will have no further exposure to possible parasites or diseases carried by the prey animal. To satisfy its hunting instincts, keep your indoor cat well supplied with catnip mice and other suitable, safe toys.

Although they are natural mousers, cats risk contracting parasites and other infections when they consume live prey. Cat food, on the other hand, is sterilized by the cooking process.

Chapter 7
Obesity: Making Fat Cats Fit

Is Your Cat Too Fat?

Obesity, the accumulation of too much body fat, is considered the number one nutritional disorder among pets in the United States. As in people, the extra poundage puts pets at higher risk for certain health conditions, such as diabetes, heart disease, lameness, and joint problems, among other ills. Experts also warn that obesity can increase

This cat is overweight, but any changes in its diet must be done gradually and should be carefully supervised by a veterinarian.

the risk of anesthesia and surgical complications. Because of the added health risks, being overweight may even contribute to a shorter lifespan in cats, just as it can for people. That's why it's so important to be able to recognize when your cat is overweight, and then take corrective action to remedy the condition.

Assessing Body Condition

How can you tell for sure if your cat needs to go on a diet? Numbers alone do not tell the whole story. Normal, fit adult cats, depending on their build and bone structure, may weigh anywhere from five to 20 pounds or more. The best way to judge whether a cat is overweight or underweight is to visually assess its body condition. But this is not as easy as it sounds. Studies have shown that a significant number of owners are poor judges of their animal's weight status. They may perceive their cat as well-fed and fit when really it is much too tubby. To make matters even more confusing, "ideal" weight varies from one individual to another, depending on a cat's breed, age, sex, and other factors. Because some breeds are heavier-boned than others, they may look stocky and chunky but still be fit. Longhaired cats also can appear to be fat when they really aren't, because their fluffy fur makes them look larger. Similarly, the slender Oriental breeds may appear too thin when really they are trim and fit for their breed standard.

If you're unsure whether your cat is at ideal weight, simply ask your veterinarian. A trained practitioner can best assess your cat's overall fitness and body condition. In general, an animal is considered too fat if it exceeds its ideal weight by 15 to 20 percent. The Ralston Purina Company, makers of Purina Cat Chow and other brand-name cat foods, has developed a nine-point Body Condition System that is widely used by veterinary practitioners to help educate pet owners on recognizing weight problems in their cats (see chart, page 142). This point system was developed and tested at the Purina Pet Care Center near St. Louis, Missouri, for the purpose of diagnosing obesity and assessing body condition.

Signs of Obesity

In general, a cat is too fat if you cannot feel its ribs without having to probe with your fingers through thick, fleshy layers. Fat cats also often have sagging, pendulous bellies, bulges around the neck, and

Visually assessing body condition is not always easy, because certain breed standards call for a slim, trim, fit cat like this one; whereas, others, like the standard for the Persian, require a round, stocky build.

heavy accumulations of fat at the base of the tail. In contrast, fit cats have a discernible waist—a slight dip in their sides just behind the ribs—when viewed from above. Their ribs can be felt easily with the fingers and have only a minimal covering of normal body fat. A cat that is too thin has visible ribs (unless it is longhaired, of course) covered by little or no fat.

Typically, too, fat cats are less active and more lethargic than fit cats. Their cumbersome body makes getting around more difficult for them. This decline in exercise and normal activity only exacerbates their overweight problem and contributes to joint stiffness and stress already

This Abyssinian mother will pass along to her kittens a genetic predisposition to be active and slender.

aggravated by excess weight. Some overweight cats even begin to experience skin and coat problems, because their decreased flexibility makes it too difficult for them to do as good a job of self-grooming. In morbidly obese animals, sores may even appear under folds of fat where the skin cannot air out properly.

Depending on the climate and environment, fat cats may even pant more, because their excess body fat makes them less tolerant to heat. Their breathing also may be noticeably more labored, because of the additional stress and pressure placed on their body organs. Because shortness of breath can also be a sign of heart problems, caused by fluid buildup in the chest cavity, have your cat examined by a veterinarian to rule out serious, underlying medical problems before putting the animal on any kind of weight-reduction program.

Causes of Obesity

Heredity: Cats get fat for basically the same reasons people do: too much food and too little exercise. However, as in people, the condition can be quite complex, and more factors than just calories can play a role in the development of the obese cat. For example, an individual's breed and genetics may predispose it to becoming a fat cat. Some active breeds, such as the Siamese and Abyssinians, are far less prone to putting on excess pounds than the more sedate felines, such as the Persians, which are well-loved for their passive, laid-back temperaments. Of course, this doesn't mean that mixed breeds are any less prone to obesity. On the contrary, almost any cat, with or without a pedigree, can become a fat cat under the right circumstances.

Lack of exercise: Available exercise opportunities make a big difference, too. Cats that go outdoors certainly expend more energy hunting prey, climbing trees, and prowling their territories. While to some this may be viewed as a plus, outdoor cats are clearly more vulnerable to numerous dangers associated with the outside world. While keeping cats indoors can help them enjoy safer, healthier, and longer lives, it's important to substitute appropriate and ample play and exercise opportunities for confined cats, particularly those living in small apartments. Helping indoor cats stay fit and trim is not difficult at all and can even be a satisfying source of pleasure for both owner and pet. For more details on this, please see the section on Exercising Your Cat (page 95).

Medical problems: As is true in people, individual metabolism and certain medical conditions that influence the way the body breaks down and uses food can contribute to obesity in cats. Most notably, these include disorders of the endocrine system or glands. *Hypothyroidism,* caused by an underactive thyroid gland, slows down the body's metabolism, causing an animal to gain weight and appear sluggish. Diabetes can also cause weight gain, but it is more commonly associated with weight loss. When evaluating cases of obesity, most veterinarians will screen for these and certain other disorders simply to rule them out, before prescribing any weight-loss program.

Overfeeding: By far, the most common cause of obesity in cats is simply the consumption of too many calories over a period of time. Many cats fed dry food free-choice regulate their own consumption and never develop a weight problem, but others will overeat if given unlimited access to too much food. If yours is one of the latter, make sure that you carefully measure out only the recommended daily ration for your cat to eat at leisure. Follow the product feeding guidelines for the amount of food you should offer your cat each day. However, keep in mind that every cat is different,

and its individual metabolic makeup ultimately determines how much food it needs each day. Closely observe your cat's condition and eating habits and make adjustments as needed.

If weight gain becomes a problem, your veterinarian may recommend that you gradually cut back the amount fed or that you consider using an alternative feeding method. For example, it may become necessary to switch from feeding free-choice to serving meals in controlled portions offered at set mealtimes. When using this method, remove any remaining food after about 30 minutes, or when your cat stops eating and walks away from its dish.

Competitive eating: In multicat households, competitive eating tends to make some cats overeat. Often, the dominant cat will gobble up its own food, then shove aside a buddy to down its portion too, just

Scratching posts and carpeted climbing trees provide indoor cats and kittens with opportunities for play and exercise.

89

Fat cats typically have bulges of fat around the face, neck, waistline, and rump.

high-fat people foods, such as french fries, cookies, potato chips, and ice cream. These are just as fattening to cats as they are to humans. If you're going to give treats, stick with the commercial cat treats made especially for the feline palate.

Age: Research has shown that cats in their middle years, between the ages of 6 and 11 years, are more likely to be fat than either younger or older cats. Kittens stay trim by expending lots of calories and energy for growth and play. To a lesser extent, young adult cats continue this energy expenditure for several years as they hunt, prowl, play, and search for mates. But for many, the middle years bring with them the middle-age spread. And as cats creep into old age, they tend to grow thinner with time, because their bodies no longer digest and use nutrients as efficiently.

to show who's boss. The obvious solution in this case is to feed cats in separate areas, and always use separate bowls, one to each cat. If necessary, supervise mealtimes to make sure each cat eats from its own bowl.

Too many treats: Some owners simply offer too much food, while others unwittingly contribute to a weight problem by feeding too many high-fat, gourmet snacks between meals. The habit of overfeeding treats commonly arises as a means of expressing affection, often because the owner has learned from his or her own life experiences to associate food with reward and love. While there is nothing wrong with giving cats occasional treats, care should be taken to restrict the amount and frequency so that a weight problem does not develop. Treats should not be fed daily, but reserved for special occasions or used sparingly as a reward. In addition, limit the portions to only a few tasty tidbits at a time. Avoid feeding

Altering: The notion that spaying the female cat or neutering the male causes them to get fat has never been proven. While experts can still say with some certainty that spaying and neutering do not *directly* cause cats to get fat, there is evidence that the absence of gonadotropic (sex) hormones may alter the body's energy or calorie requirements in some individuals. This means that, while not a direct cause of obesity, these surgeries can become influential factors in a weight problem when combined with major contributing causes, such as consistent overfeeding. For this reason, responsible owners

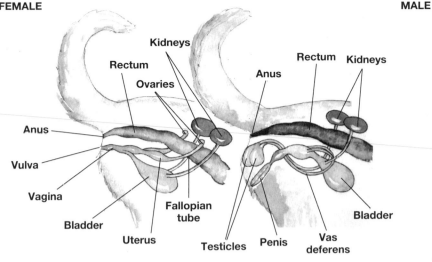

FEMALE   **MALE**

Kidneys

Rectum

Ovaries

Rectum   Kidneys

Anus

Anus

Vulva

Vagina

Fallopian
tube

Bladder

Bladder

Uterus

Testicles   Penis   Vas
deferens

Spaying removes a female cat's ovaries, tubes, and uterus so that she cannot have kittens. Neutering sterilizes the male cat and reduces or eliminates undesirable urine spraying behaviors. Neither spaying nor neutering directly causes cats to become fat.

need to be aware of this potential so they can watch for signs of weight gain following the operations and, if necessary, adjust their cats' caloric intake accordingly. Always consult a veterinarian first before putting a cat on any special diet, including one designed for weight loss.

Too much of a too-rich diet: The type of food fed to a cat also influences weight. Many of the so-called "premium" cat foods are more appropriately termed *energy-dense*, meaning that their richer ingredient mix delivers more calories and energy per serving. Often, they are designed to be more digestible, which means that the cat can use more of the food's nutrient value from smaller portions. This can be a plus, as long as you offer the portions recommended on the package label. However, too many owners who switch to premium foods inadvertently end up

overfeeding their pets. This is because they often fail to consult the new package's feeding guidelines and continue to offer the same size portions they've become accustomed to putting in the bowl each day. And because many premium foods are designed to be highly palatable, some cats tend to eat what's offered with great gusto, simply because the food tastes good. This, of course, tempts their delighted owners to indulge them even more, until overeating and overfeeding become routine.

Because feeding directions can vary significantly from one product to another, always read the feeding guidelines on the package before offering any new food product to your cat. If your cat starts to gain weight on any food, whether premium or not, check the guidelines to make sure you're feeding the recommended daily amount. If you

While cats kept indoors are safe from the hazards lurking outdoors, they risk not getting enough exercise unless you provide toys and opportunity for interactive play.

determine that you're overfeeding, cut back gradually to the recommended portions.

Weight-Loss Formula Cat Foods

"Light" Foods

Historically, the words *light, lean, reduced,* and similar designations have had little regulatory meaning in the pet food industry. Fortunately, this is due to change as soon as states begin to implement AAFCO's new regulations regarding such dietary claims. Until recently, AAFCO recommendations required a "light cat food" to deliver at least 15 percent less energy than the company's regular product. The problem with this definition was that it offered no consistency from one manufacturer to another. For example, a light food produced by one manufacturer could contain more calories than a regular food made by a different manufacturer.

To remedy this, AAFCO agreed on new regulations in late 1996 intended to standardize dietary claims on pet food labels so that consumers will be better able to compare like products made by different manufacturers.

Most states are expected to adopt the new standardized regulations, which will require that cat food products claiming to be "light," "lite," or "low calorie" meet specific calorie maximum amounts based on the weight of the contents—not the volume—and on the percentage of moisture in the product. While products claiming to have "less calories" or "reduced calories" won't be held to the same calorie counts as "lite" or "low calorie" foods, they will have to state and substantiate the percentage of reduction along with a basis of comparison. The new guidelines will be included in upcoming editions of AAFCO's *Official Publication.*

About Calorie Content Statements

Although not required on pet food labels that make no calorie-related claims, calorie content statements that are used on products claiming to be "light, "lite," "low calorie," "less calories," or "reduced calories" must be substantiated according to AAFCO's regulations. The statement has to appear on the label distinctly apart from the guaranteed analysis. The number of calories also must be measured in terms of metabolizable energy (ME) and expressed in kilocalories per kilogram (kcal/kg). Other common units of measurement, such as kilocalories per cup or pound, may be used in addition to the mandatory kcal/kg. ME, or the amount of energy actually used or metabolized by the animal, can be substantiated by calculation or by feeding trials.

"Low Fat" Foods

Cat foods that bear "lean" or "low fat" claims must meet certain maximum crude fat percentages based on the product's moisture content, according to AAFCO's new guidelines. Such products also have to express minimum and maximum crude fat guarantees in the guaranteed analysis section of the label. Products claiming to contain "less fat" or "reduced fat" must state similar guarantees, plus the percentage of reduction along with a basis of comparison.

Veterinary-Dispensed Weight-Loss Diets

Although an obese cat needs fewer calories and fats, it still requires adequate amounts of protein, vitamins, and minerals to maintain good health. The ideal weight-reduction formula is designed to provide all of these essential nutrients while restricting caloric intake. Calories come primarily from proteins, carbohydrates, and fats, so the amounts of these ingredients must be carefully controlled. Because of the restricted amounts of certain ingredients, weight-reduc-

tion formulas are not appropriate diets for cats of all life stages. The reduced energy value of weight-reduction foods simply cannot meet the extra needs of growing kittens and pregnant or nursing queens, for example. Nor are they necessarily suitable as daily rations for adult, nonbreeding cats that do not have a weight problem or that have other medical problems. For these reasons, many manufacturers design their weight-loss products as therapeutic diets, to be dispensed through veterinarians. This way, the veterinarian can evaluate the need for the special diet and properly supervise and monitor the cat's weight-loss progress.

Therapeutic weight-loss cat foods are usually formulated to be relatively low in calories and fat, but higher in fiber. Because fiber is poorly digestible, it delivers fewer calories. The increased amount of dietary crude fiber in these formulas may also help promote a feeling of fullness in the cat so that it doesn't feel deprived and hungry while on the weight-loss program. However, the problem with more fiber is that it produces greater stool volume.

Putting a Cat on a Diet

The owner who arbitrarily reduces a cat's rations or suddenly switches the cat to a weight-loss diet without first consulting a veterinarian is asking for trouble. An abrupt change in

Never put a fat cat on a crash diet. Safe weight loss must be gradual and medically supervised to avoid serious complications.

diet may make the cat stop eating altogether, leading to serious illness. All changes in diet must be made gradually over a period of one or two weeks by adding and mixing increasing amounts of the new food to decreasing portions of the old food until the switch is complete.

Not only must dietary changes be gradual, but the rate of weight loss for an obese cat must be gradual, too, and carefully supervised by a medical professional. One pound equals a large percentage of a cat's total body weight. So weight loss must be slow—ounce by ounce—to be safe, sometimes taking many months. Too-rapid weight loss, or "crash" diets, can be harmful, resulting in tissue wasting or causing a condition called *hepatic lipidosis,* also known as fatty liver disease. As the name implies, fatty liver disease develops when too much fat (lipids) builds up in the liver's cells. The disorder is sometimes seen when a cat, particularly a heavyset feline, suddenly stops eating, and, if the restricted intake is allowed to continue, fat begins to accumulate in

the liver. Left untreated, the condition can quickly become life-threatening, which is why loss of appetite in the cat should *never* be ignored. Treatment consists of getting the cat to eat again as soon as possible, whether it be by forced oral feeding or by intravenous feeding.

The key to success in any feline weight-loss program is owner compliance. The owner must first recognize that the cat is overweight and then be willing to follow a veterinarian's instructions to the letter. From the veterinarian's standpoint, modifying the owner's feeding behavior is sometimes as big a part of the program as prescribing and supervising a proper diet. For example, the owner who reinforces the human-animal bond by offering too many rich treats must learn to replace this habit with other reward actions, such as praise, petting, and grooming. Interestingly, studies show a correlation among overweight pets and overweight owners, suggesting that learned associations linking food offerings with affection may be at work, along with other complex psychological factors.

During treatment, the veterinarian may ask the owner to weigh the cat weekly and keep a detailed record of the type and amounts of all food given. This helps to adjust the weight-loss rate as needed. Weighing a cat can be tricky, because most refuse to stand or sit on the scales long enough for you to get a good reading. The easiest way to accomplish "weighing-in" at home is to weigh yourself first on a reliable bathroom scale. Then, hold the cat in your arms and step on the scale a second time. Subtracting your weight will give you the cat's weight.

While the cat is on the weight-loss diet, it is best to cut out *all* treats and table scraps; however, if you insist on offering them, be sure to include them in your weekly log. Avoid offering food in bulk, as in filling a self-feeder or a large bowl full of several meal portions at one time. If your cat already has a problem self-regulating its food intake, bulk feeding indiscriminate portions will only encourage overeating and make the problem worse. Free-choice feeding of dry rations is OK, if that is the way your cat is used to being fed, but the key is to measure and leave out only the recommended amount per day, if feeding once a day, or per serving, if feeding at multiple mealtime intervals. That way, your cat can nibble at will, but when the last bit of food is gone from the bowl, it will have eaten only the daily ration or a controlled-portion serving, whichever is the case.

If you have more than one cat, free-choice feeding can present some special problems, since cats in the same household tend to swap and share bowls and eat each other's food. To accommodate one on a special diet, it may be necessary to reconsider how you feed all of your cats, or at least to feed the one on the special diet separately and restrict its access to the other

cats' food (see page 64). Otherwise, it will certainly move over to a buddy's bowl to eat more. In addition, if you allow your cat to go outdoors, supervise its activities so that it won't hunt and scavenge for food, or seek out another meal at a nearby neighbor's house. This may mean keeping the cat in a screened enclosure, such as a porch, or teaching it to walk on a leash. (For leash-training tips, see page 98.)

Bulk feeders and waterers are handy for times when you need to be away overnight. Used routinely, however, bulk feeding sometimes encourages overeating and can result in an overweight cat.

Exercising Your Cat

As with human weight-loss programs, exercise is also an important factor in successfully slimming down the tubby tabby. Most obese cats lead sedentary lives. This may be due partly to the cat's personality, or it may be a direct result of limited exercise opportunities available in its environment. For example, the apartment-confined cat has little territory to defend and less

spend short periods each day letting your cat stalk and chase the flying lure. Because strings, sparklers, and feathers can be hazardous to cats if chewed and swallowed, always store this type of toy in a closet, safely out of your cat's reach, when you are not present to supervise play. Any toy with string or yarn is especially dangerous if a cat is left unsupervised with it. The string can get wrapped around the neck or a limb and cause choking or cut off the circulation. Also, if swallowed, string or yarn can amass in the intestines and cause a life-threatening condition called *string enteritis* (see page 110).

Other Cat Toys

Some inexpensive items provide good exercise and fun for cats, including Ping-Pong balls, golf balls, tennis balls, and a cardboard box with cut-out peep holes. All cats love to play hide-and-seek in paper grocery bags, but avoid plastic bags because cats, like children, may suffocate in them. When choosing cat toys, always consider safety. Select only sturdy toys that won't disintegrate after the first few mock attacks. Remove tied-on bells, plastic eyes, button noses, and dangling strings that your cat could tear off and swallow or choke on during play. Avoid items small enough to be swallowed, such as buttons, hair pins, rubber bands, wire bread-wrapper ties, paper clips, wadded cellophane, and candy wrappers.

Interactive play is a fun way to exercise your indoor cat and strengthen the human-animal bond. It's also a good opportunity to observe your cat's innate prey-catching behaviors, the same ones it would use when hunting live prey.

room to romp. Certainly, this statement is not meant to imply that confining cats indoors is a bad idea. On the contrary, keeping cats indoors is preferable because they live longer, healthier lives. Indoor cats are less likely to be exposed to parasites or disease, injured in cat fights, hit by cars, attacked by dogs, poisoned by spilled chemicals, or harmed by cruel people. However, the owner of an indoor cat needs to devise ample exercise opportunities by playing with the cat more and by installing carpeted climbing trees.

Interactive Toys

Interactive play with your cat can be fun for you and healthy for your cat. The time you enjoy together in this way also helps strengthen the human/animal bond. Use one of those fishing-pole-style toys with a feather, pompom, or sparkler lure attached on the end of a string and

Catnip

Catnip mice, catnip sacks, and other catnip-scented toys offer another good way to enliven the sedentary feline's life. A member of the mint family, catnip is a perennial herb you can grow indoors or outdoors for your cat's enjoyment. Pet stores usually sell it in dried, chopped-leaf form, which you can use to make and stuff your own catnip sacks. Or simply rub the leaves over the scratching post, and watch your cat go into a climbing frenzy.

Many cats go wild over catnip, rolling ecstatically and rubbing their faces in the dried leaves or a scented toy. After a brief burst of playful energy, they lie sprawled on their backs in a trancelike, euphoric state, as if drunk, purring loudly and contentedly. The substance in the plant that causes this reaction is called *nepetalactone.* The effect wears off in a short time, and the herb is not thought to be addictive or harmful to domestic cats. However, not all cats experience this catnip high. About half lack the gene that makes them respond to the plant's intoxicating effects and will show no marked reaction when exposed to it.

Give Your Cat a Playmate

Another good way to give your cat exercise is to provide it with a live-in playmate. If you can afford it, keeping two cats instead of one helps ensure that a single feline left at home alone all day does not become bored and lonely. Despite

Two cats in the house will romp and play together and provide one another with exercise and entertainment.

their aloof reputations, cats are highly social animals, and most enjoy the companionship of their own kind, as long as they are properly introduced and socialized. After establishing their own household hierarchy, most cat companions will play together, sleep together, and even groom each other.

When selecting a second cat, stick with the same or similar breed, if yours is a purebred. You want both cats to have similar temperaments in terms of their activity level and need for attention.

If you already have an adult cat, bringing a new kitten into its territory must be managed carefully. Before exposing any newcomer to your resident cat, have it checked by a veterinarian and tested for disease, especially feline leukemia virus (FeLV) and feline immunodeficiency virus (FIV). While awaiting the test results, keep the new arrival isolated from other pets, in a separate room or in a pen. This also allows time for the house smell to settle on the newcomer, which may help make the introductions less threatening. It's usually easier to introduce a kitten, rather than a grown cat, into a home that already has a feline. After a few days, remove the new cat from its separate quarters for awhile and let the resident cat go in and sniff the new scent. When the time seems right, allow the two to see each other, but supervise all contact for the first few weeks. Gradually increase the exposure until the cats accept each other and learn to coexist peaceably.

Don't be dismayed if it takes as long as a month for the animals to accept each other and settle down. Cats are territorial, and adding a newcomer means new boundaries must be set. In time, the tension usually disappears. However, cats, like people, are individuals, and occasionally two turn out to be simply incompatible. Be prepared for this outcome, just in case. Before adopting or buying a second cat, agree on a plan for its return to the original owner in the event that things don't work out in the new home.

Taking Your Cat for Walks

Another good way to exercise your indoor cat and allow it to safely experience the outdoors is to take it for walks on a leash. As odd as the idea may seem, many cats, with patience and perseverance, can learn to enjoy walking on a leash. Just don't expect them to heel with precision by your side the way a trained dog does. Some cats take to walking on a leash better than others, and those that do generally prefer to lead the way. Much depends on individual temperament. And, of course, there will always be certain individuals who simply won't tolerate the notion at all.

To determine whether your cat will adapt to leash walking, start by selecting an adjustable nylon or leather cat harness and a lightweight leash. Most pet supply stores and catalogs market figure-eight harnesses designed specifically to restrain cats so they can't slip free and escape. Never use a choker collar designed for dogs on a cat. Also, avoid dog harnesses, as cats can easily slip out of them and run away from you.

To begin leash training, accustom the cat to the harness by putting it on when you're home to supervise. Let the cat drag the leash freely

With patience, some cats can be trained to walk on a leash. This provides exercise and an opportunity for your cat to safely experience the outdoors under your supervision.

behind it, but don't leave the cat unattended while doing this because it might get entangled or accidentally hang itself. After the cat is used to wearing the equipment, begin leading it about indoors on the leash. The best way to accomplish this is to use a pull toy for enticement, gently coaxing the cat to follow you on the leash for short distances. Praise the cat lavishly when it goes in the desired direction. Confine your practice sessions indoors until your cat walks comfortably with you on a leash throughout the house. Only then should you venture outside for short walks, making sure to select a quiet, secluded area so that your cat won't be frightened by unfamiliar sights and sounds. Until your cat adjusts to the outdoors, take along a pet carrier. That way, if something frightens the cat and causes it to struggle on the leash, you can pop it into its carrier for safety. The continement of the carrier will also serve to calm a scared cat and make it feel more secure.

Chapter 8

Functions and Dysfunctions of the Feline Digestive System

The Mouth

Although not truly a part of the cat's digestive system, the mouth is where predigestion of food begins. The cat uses its teeth to tear and grind its food into smaller bits. Saliva from glands inside the mouth helps soften the food for swallowing and lubricate its passage down the throat and into the stomach. A problem that impairs either of these important functions, whether it be an abscessed tooth or a tumor of the salivary glands, can seriously impede a cat's ability to chew and swallow its daily rations. Inflamed gums or mouth ulcers can also make eating unpleasant enough for a cat to go off its feed. If your cat suddenly stops eating or refuses food for no apparent reason, don't delay in getting the cause checked out. A visit to the veterinarian can determine whether dental or medical care is in order.

Foreign Objects in the Mouth

Likewise, a foreign object, such as a pin or a staple, lodged in the throat or mouth can prevent the cat from eating. Depending on the size and position of the object, the cat may not appear to be in obvious distress, but it may stop eating. However, if the animal is salivating, gagging, and pawing at its mouth, it may be choking on a foreign object in its mouth or feeling severe discomfort. To attempt first aid, open the mouth, try to pull out the tongue, if you can do so safely, and look down the throat. If you can see an obstructing object, use tweezers to attempt to gently extract it. If the object seems stuck and will not readily budge, make no further attempt to dislodge it without veterinary assistance. You may do more harm than good. Seek medical attention immediately.

The Tongue and Taste Buds

The cat's sandpaper rough, raspy tongue is well-suited to scrubbing fur and feathers from its live prey, then licking the bones clean afterward. The tongue also is covered by an array of specialized cells or taste buds designed to detect the various chemical components of foods as the saliva in the mouth dissolves them. Taste tests suggest that cats can distinguish between salty or sour foods, but they cannot taste simple sugars. This means that cats don't crave sweets the way some people do. Their preference, of course, is meat (the smellier the better) served at room temperature (or even better, at the body temperature of small prey animals). Besides tasting, the tongue acts as a spoon for ladling liquids into the mouth. It also serves to propel food to the back of the mouth, where it is swallowed and conveyed to the stomach for digestion.

The Gastrointestinal Tract

Esophagus

From the mouth, swallowed food moves down the throat in a muscular tube called the *esophagus* until it reaches the stomach. Automatic muscle contractions in this tube propel the food to its destination. As food is swallowed, the *epiglottis,* a tissue flap in the back of the mouth, closes over another tube in the throat, called the *trachea,* commonly known as the windpipe, to prevent food or liquid from entering

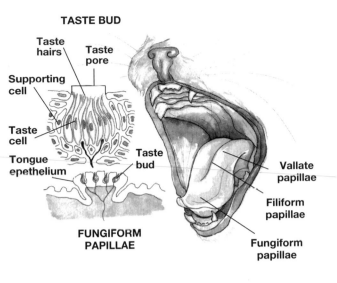

TASTE BUD

Taste hairs · Taste pore · Supporting cell · Taste cell · Tongue epethelium · Taste bud · **FUNGIFORM PAPILLAE** · Vallate papillae · Filiform papillae · Fungiform papillae

the lungs. Because air enroute to the lungs and food enroute to the stomach cross at this junction, the swallowing mechanism must function with precision. Serious consequences, such as potentially fatal pneumonia, can result if food or other foreign material is accidentally aspirated into the lungs.

This is of particular concern when administering liquid foods or medications to a cat by mouth, for example. To properly administer liquids, tilt the head back slightly, insert an eyedropper or syringe (without the needle) into the corner of the mouth and gently squirt or squeeze in a few drops at a time. To help prevent the cat from accidentally inhaling the liquid, take care not to empty the contents into the cat's mouth too quickly or too forcefully. Hold the mouth shut and allow the cat time to swallow, stroking the throat to encourage it to do so.

The mouth is where predigestion begins. The feline tongue is covered with taste buds that can detect salty and sour flavors, but not simple sugars.

The cat's digestive tract is essentially a long tube that starts at the mouth and ends at the anus. Its function is to break down food into nutrients that the body can use.

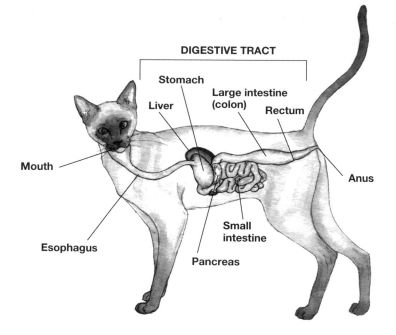

DIGESTIVE TRACT

Stomach

Liver

Large intestine (colon)

Rectum

Mouth

Anus

Small intestine

Esophagus

Pancreas

Stomach

When food reaches the stomach, powerful gastric juices immediately set to work dissolving and digesting it. These acidic juices are produced and controlled by a complex sequence of neural and hormonal interactions that are stimulated when the cat gets its first whiff of food. The stomach's muscular walls repeatedly contract to mix and mash these juicy enzymes with the food.

Small Intestine

From the stomach, digested food empties into the small intestine at a controlled rate. Here, protein is reduced to amino acids; fats break down into fatty acids, and so forth. As bile from the liver and pancreatic juices from the pancreas help complete this phase of the digestion process, nutrients are absorbed through the intestinal wall into the bloodstream.

Large Intestine

From the small intestine, food passes into the large intestine, or *colon,* where colonies of good bacteria reside to help finish fermenting and breaking down the remaining food. These bacteria are also essential to the production of certain vitamins, and long-term use of antibiotics can kill them off, seriously interfering with this important function. The *rectum,* which is part of the large intestine, collects and holds fecal waste for elimination through the *anus.*

Other Organs of the Digestive System

Pancreas

This small but vital organ secretes digestive enzymes that enter the small intestine through the pancreatic duct. Its best-known function is the production of *insulin,* an important chemical that helps regulate sugar metabolism. When the pancreas fails to produce sufficient amounts of insulin, sugar builds up in the blood, resulting in the disease called *diabetes.* Diabetes is incurable, but it can be controlled by sound dietary management and insulin replacement therapy. Left untreated, the disease can lead to coma and death. Symptoms of diabetes may include excessive thirst, excessive urination, and weight loss.

Liver

The liver performs many functions vital to the digestion and metabolism of food nutrients, and the body cannot live without this important organ. It manufactures several enzymes and hormones and is involved in the storage and synthesis of sugars and proteins. The organ's production of *bile* aids in the proper absorption of fats. The liver also helps break down and detoxify waste products and drugs. Despite this amazing ability, the liver can be seriously damaged by certain drugs and poisons consumed by a cat. Acetaminophen, ibuprofen, and aspirin are just a few of the common household medications that can cause liver damage or failure if a cat accidentally ingests them (see page 134). Infectious diseases and parasites can also impair liver function.

In some cases, lack of food for too long a period, or even too-rapid weight loss, can have serious consequences in the form of *hepatic lipidosis,* also called *fatty liver disease* (see page 94). To avoid these consequences when switching foods or putting an overweight cat on a diet, it is especially important to make changes *gradually,* reducing food portions over a period of time as needed, and having the cat's weight-loss progress monitored closely by a veterinarian. Symptoms of liver dysfunction include weight loss, appetite loss, vomiting, diarrhea, lethargy, a bloated abdomen, and jaundice (yellowed mucous membranes). Treatment of liver disease depends on the diagnosis and may include special dietary management.

Disorders of the Digestive System

Vomiting and Diarrhea

Occasional or intermittent vomiting can result from something as simple as eating grass, overeating, eating too fast, or accumulating hair balls in the stomach. Often, this is no cause for concern unless it becomes too frequent. Similarly, occasional diarrhea may occur with sudden changes in the cat's diet. But these symptoms can also be due to something more serious, such as internal parasite infestation, tumors, chronic intestinal disease, and kidney or liver disease. Bacterial or viral disease, intestinal obstructions, or accidental poisonings can all produce the sudden onset of vomiting or diarrhea. Whatever the cause, persistent or severe vomiting or diarrhea can quickly lead to excessive fluid loss and potentially fatal dehydration if left untreated. Such symptoms are especially alarming when seen in kittens. Because dehydration can occur within a matter of hours in a kitten's smaller body, *immediate* medical attention is a must. Even with adult cats, consult a veterinarian right away when symptoms seem severe or persistent. Do not wait to see if the symptoms will disappear on their own.

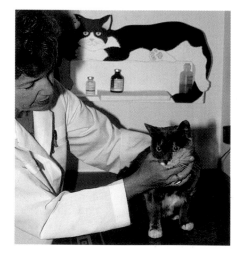

Regular check-ups and annual vaccinations will help prevent infectious diseases and other health problems in your cat.

To aid the veterinarian's diagnosis, note the appearance and frequency of the vomiting or diarrhea, along with any other differences in your cat's behavior or eating patterns that you have observed. For example, does the cat vomit continuously or intermittently? If intermittently, how often? Does the cat eat, then throw up its food whole immediately afterward? Does the vomit look like partially digested food, or is it a clear, frothy fluid? Can you see any blood in the vomit or stools? Most important, has the cat quit eating altogether and, if so, for how long?

Although the words are often used interchangeably, *regurgitation* differs technically from *vomiting*. The act of regurgitation brings up undigested food shortly after eating. Vomiting is a more forceful, retching expulsion of partially digested food that is generally sour-smelling and bile-coated. From a diagnostic standpoint, these distinctions are important for the veterinarian to know, should you observe them in your cat. For example, if a cat has a blockage that prevents the passage of food into the stomach, it may regurgitate whole, undigested food immediately after eating.

Infectious Diseases

While many ailments can strike cats, the most common viral diseases with attendant vomiting and diarrhea include feline panleukopenia virus (FPV) and feline infectious peritonitis (FIP). In addition, the feline immunodeficiency virus (FIV) often is accompanied by chronic diarrhea. Symptoms of these illnesses are as follows:

- **FPV,** also called feline infectious enteritis and feline distemper, attacks the lining of the small intestine, typically causing the afflicted cat to exhibit a painful abdomen or cry out pitifully when touched. The word *enteritis* means irritation or inflammation of the small intestine. Symptoms include fever, depression, appetite loss, and vomiting of yellow bile. Without early treatment, an infected cat becomes desperately ill. Annual vaccination effectively prevents this devastating and usually fatal disease. For kittens, initial immunity is established through a series of injections administered at 6-8 weeks, 10-12 weeks, and 16 weeks. Because immunity tends to wane over time, annual booster shots are strongly recommended.

- **FIP** is caused by a coronavirus that sets up an inflammatory response in the body's blood vessels and tissues. The disease is characterized as being either "wet" or "dry." In the wet form, fluid builds up in the cat's chest and abdomen. Symptoms include a swollen belly, labored breathing, and extreme lethargy. The dry form progresses more slowly, is difficult to diagnose, and affects many more organs, including the pancreas, liver, kidneys, brain, and eyes. Once symptoms appear, the illness is nearly always fatal. It strikes primarily young and old cats, or those debilitated by other diseases. A vaccine for FIP became available in 1991 and is administered by nose drops.

- **FIV,** also called "feline AIDS," appears to be transmitted among cats primarily through bites. Because this particular virus is specific to the feline species, it does *not* cause AIDS in humans, and an infected cat poses *no* known threat to human health. Free-roaming cats, especially ones that are not spayed or neutered, are at greatest risk of contracting and spreading the disease among other cats. This is because free-roaming intact animals tend to engage frequently in fights over territory or mates, and thus are more likely to sustain bite wounds. Once contracted, the disease can persist for months or even years before the cat's weakening immune system finally succumbs to some opportunistic infection. Symptoms vary widely but often include persistent diarrhea, chronic infections, appetite loss, weight loss, gingivitis (inflamed gums), mouth ulcers, and tooth loss. The latter symptoms may make eating more difficult for the sick cat, necessitating a soft diet. No approved vaccine is available yet for FIV. To date, the best prevention is simply keeping cats safely indoors, thereby avoiding contact with infected free-roaming felines.

Salmonella Infection

Most people hear warnings about this bacterial disease at Thanksgiving, when thawing, cooking, cutting, and serving the holiday turkey, if done improperly, can contribute to spreading the disease. Fortunately, healthy cats kept in clean conditions and properly fed rarely fall victim to *Salmonella* infection. When contracted, however, the disease is capable of producing enteritis in the species with attendant diarrhea, ranging from mild to severe. However, many afflicted cats may show no symptoms at all, but may shed the bacteria in their feces. Mention of this here is important because the infection can be transmitted to human beings.

Like people, cats can contract this disease from eating raw or undercooked meat. They also can contract the disease from eating raw eggs or infected wild prey. To help prevent the disease, simply avoid offering or exposing your pet to these raw food sources. If you must feed an occasional meat or egg, make sure they are cooked, and not raw or rare. Also, don't allow cats to lick unwashed platters or cutting boards where raw meats have been thawed or chopped. Discard empty food wrappers or containers in a tightly covered trash can where cats can't get at them. To avoid exposing cats to diseases and parasites carried by wild prey, restrict their hunting by keeping cats safely indoors. Also, always practice good hygiene, keep kitty's quarters sanitary, and wash your hands after cleaning litter boxes or handling any sick cat, particularly one suffering from diarrhea of unknown cause.

Constipation

While constipation is less likely to be life threatening than diarrhea and the accompanying dehydration, a chronic problem can be a good indication of a more serious underlying condition. Most cats pass one or two normal, brown stools per day. Improper diet or lack of exercise can contribute to stools that are hard and difficult to pass, resulting in constipation. (See the chart on page 108 for what to look for in stool appearance and consistency.) Other possible causes include medications, colon disease, neurological disorders, and thyroid dysfunction. Bowel obstructions from impacted hair balls or foreign material may also produce symptoms of constipation.

If the cat appears to strain in an attempt to defecate and makes

Straining to urinate is often mistaken for constipation. If you notice your cat visiting the litter box frequently, urinating in unusual places, or passing blood, suspect feline lower urinary tract disorder and seek veterinary care immediately.

frequent visits to the litter box, consult a veterinarian immediately. The problem may not be constipation at all. It is often easy to confuse what looks like constipation with feline lower urinary tract disorder (FLUTD), also known as feline urologic syndrome (FUS). In FLUTD, the outlet from the bladder, the *urethra,* is either fully or partially blocked by solidified mineral crystals. If the blockage prevents the cat from passing its urine, the waste may back up in the system and permanently damage the kidneys or cause death (see page 114).

Gastritis and Enteritis

Typically brought on by bouts of dietary indiscretion, *gastritis,* or inflammation of the stomach lining, and *enteritis,* inflammation of the small intestine, usually respond favorably to proper diet (see page 120) and medication, depending upon the cause. These conditions are more likely to be seen in free-roaming cats than in cats kept strictly indoors. This is because cats allowed outdoors generally have more opportunity to eat spoiled foods from garbage bins or to come in contact with chemical irritants. Consuming nonfood garbage, such as plastic wrap, bones, or aluminum foil may also contribute to a gastrointestinal episode, or even cause a blockage. Certain viral infections, such as feline panleukopenia virus (FPV), also result in enteritis, as previously discussed. The principal symptom is vomiting, with or with-

Cats allowed to roam freely and forage from garbage cans are more likely to experience bouts of gastritis or enteritis from eating spoiled food, bones, plastic wrap, or contaminates.

out diarrhea. To help prevent these episodes, have all cats vaccinated and keep tight-fitting lids on all trash bins, indoors and outdoors. The latter precaution prevents foraging cats from getting sickened by rancid foodstuffs or injured by discarded razor blades, broken glass, or jagged tin can edges.

Colitis

Unlike gastritis and enteritis, there is often no known cause for *colitis,* or inflammation of the colon, or large intestine. It is sometimes seen as a complication of feline leukemia virus. Symptoms may include diarrhea, flatulence, or the passage of small, frequent stools streaked with blood or mucus. Treatment may include long-term dietary management with a high-fiber therapeutic food (see pages 13 and 120).

Parasites

The most common internal parasites that plague cats include roundworms, hookworms, and tapeworms, but there are many others. Many of these organisms live in

Stool Appearance and Consistency: What to Look For

Brown, solidly formed	Normal stool, usually one or two per day passed
Dark, hard, dry fecal balls	Indicates constipation
Soft, bulky, unformed	Suggests overfeeding or feeding high-fiber food
Light-colored or discolored	May indicate possible liver disease, malabsorption, infection
Black, tarry stools or visible blood	Indicates intestinal bleeding or infectious disease
Putrid or rancid smelling	Suggests infection or malabsorption disorder
Watery, foamy	Suggests bowel irritation, infection, malabsorption

the gastrointestinal tract, robbing the cat of valuable nutrients and producing symptoms of vomiting, diarrhea, and anemia. Their presence can sometimes result in organ damage and can leave the cat weakened and vulnerable to disease and infections.

An infected queen can pass certain worms to her kittens through the placenta and through the breast milk. This is why a kitten's first visit to the veterinarian should include a stool analysis, which unveils the presence of most worms. Because deworming drugs can cause toxic reactions, they should be administered only under veterinary supervision.

Kittens get roundworms from their infected mothers or through contact with contaminated cat feces. Signs include vomiting, diarrhea, weight loss, a potbellied appearance, and overall poor condition. Roundworms passed in vomit or stool look like white, wriggling spaghetti strands.

Hookworms, more prevalent in hot, humid areas, are picked up from soil infested with the larvae. Symptoms include anemia, diarrhea, weight loss, and black, tarry stools. Liver flukes, also more common in warmer regions, can be ingested by eating infected prey and can cause liver problems. Cats allowed outdoors should be checked for these parasites during their annual physical checkups.

Tapeworms, the most common internal parasites found in adult cats, are transmitted by rodents and fleas. During grooming, cats ingest fleas, which often carry immature tapeworms. The tapeworm larvae mature inside the cat's intestines, feeding on nutrients within and growing into long, segmented strands. When fresh segments break off and are passed in the stool, they look like grains of wriggling, white rice. Some segments may stick to the hair around the anus and, when dry, they look like tiny seeds. Left untreated, tapeworms can rob the cat of important nutrients, but rarely cause any outward clinical signs. For effective treatment, combine deworming agents with appropriate flea control measures.

Toxoplasma gondii, the organism that causes toxoplasmosis (see page 80), can lead to liver damage in the cat, although the parasitic infection itself rarely produces any noticeable symptoms. To avoid it, never feed your cat raw or undercooked meat. Overall, parasite prevention includes keeping cats indoors, discouraging predation, maintaining good sanitation, and controlling fleas, lice, cockroaches, mosquitoes, and other vermin.

Intestinal Obstructions

Hair Balls

Occasionally, cats spit up tubular masses of ingested hair, called hair balls. Before the cat vomits a hair ball, it will typically crouch, swallow repeatedly, retch, and wheeze in a dry, hacking manner. This is known as the hair ball cough. Except for the

During self-grooming, cats can ingest fleas hiding in their fur. Fleas carry tapeworm larvae, which mature into adult parasites inside the cat's intestinal tract.

mess on your rug, vomiting a hair ball is usually no cause for concern, unless it becomes too frequent.

These masses of swallowed hair accumulate in the stomach as the cat grooms itself. Normally, hair balls move through the digestive tract without causing problems and get eliminated along with other solid wastes in the usual way. Sometimes, however, a hair ball gets too large and may partially or completely obstruct the bowel, requiring immediate medical attention. An enema or even surgery may be necessary to remove the obstruction. Signs of such a blockage include frequent vomiting and refusal to eat. Left untreated, a blockage of this nature can become life-threatening.

Hair ball problems occur more frequently in longhaired cats, but

Cats are often observed grazing on grass, which may provide necessary roughage and help purge their system of excess swallowed hair.

shorthaired breeds also suffer from them. If you notice your cat crouching and producing the hair ball cough without expelling any hair mass, administer one of various petrolatum-based hair ball remedies available at pet stores and veterinarians' offices. Or dab some plain Vaseline (petroleum jelly) on your cat's paw to lick off. These products help lubricate the hair mass so that it expels more easily. But avoid using them excessively. Too-frequent use, even as often as a weekly dose, of petrolatum products may interfere with the absorp-

Regular grooming is the best and least expensive way to prevent hair balls.

tion of fat-soluble vitamins A, D, E, and K. Also, avoid using mineral oil as a laxative or hair ball remedy, as this liquid can be easily aspirated into the lungs.

Grass also seems to act as a purgative to help cats expel excess hair from the stomach. Indoor cats enjoy having their own fresh supply grown especially for them, and most pet stores sell grass kits for this purpose.

By far the most efficient and least expensive way to prevent hair balls is simply to groom your cat regularly. In longhaired breeds, daily grooming is essential for preventing unsightly mats and tangles. Shorthaired cats benefit from at least a weekly brushing. Regular brushing and combing helps remove the dead hair the cat would otherwise swallow as it self-grooms.

String Enteritis

Another common obstruction occurs when a cat is allowed to play with string, thread, or yarns and swallows the material. Once a cat starts chewing and swallowing string or yarn, a considerable amount may amass in the digestive tract and cause life-threatening blockages or perforations. If you come home to find your cat with a piece of string hanging out of its mouth, *resist the temptation* to pull it out. Pulling on the dangling end can actually cause more serious, even fatal, injury, if the string has already wound its way into the intestinal tract. Seek veterinary help

Yarn and string make dangerous cat toys. Never allow your cat to play with or have access to such items without close and constant supervision.

immediately. Surgery may be required to remove the foreign matter from the gut.

Prevention is simple. Avoid allowing your cat access to yarn balls, threaded spools, or string of any kind. Supervise all access to fishing-pole-style toys with feathers, sparklers, and lures tied to a stringed pole. These interactive toys provide great exercise, but the string feature can lead to accidental strangulation or tying off of a limb, as well as accidental ingestion, if the cat is allowed unsupervised access to the item. Shut these toys safely in a closet or cabinet when you're not playing with your cat. Also, be careful of braided rugs or knitted afghans that might unravel if the cat starts playing with a loose end.

At Christmas, avoid decorating the tree with garland and tinsel. Cats can't resist the shiny foil strands dangling from the lower branches. Inevitably, they will pull them off and eat them. Although not toxic, swallowed garland, tinsel, angel hair, and even gift wrapping ribbon can cause a serious intestinal obstruction, just as any other string-like material can.

Chapter 9

Special Problems, Special Diets

Homemade Diets versus Commercial Foods

Considering the difficulty we humans have making sure we include enough fruits and vegetables and limit the fats and sugars in our diets, wouldn't it be nice if we could pour our meals out of a bag or a can and be guaranteed of complete and balanced nutrition? That's what commercial cat foods do. They eliminate the nutrition guesswork for cat owners and handily package adequate amounts of amino acids, proteins, fats, vitamins, and minerals for the average feline.

Still, some people, concerned about chemical additives and preservatives and the overall safety of commercial food supplies, may consider turning to home-cooked meals for their cats. But just because you can oversee the ingredients and the preparation of a home-cooked meal, does that make it any healthier for your cat? Not necessarily. In fact, just the opposite may be true. While home-cooked recipes may seem to offer a reasonable and natural alternative diet, most fall far short of delivering all the nutrients a cat really needs to stay healthy. Constructing a balanced meal from scratch that meets the feline's specific nutritional needs is actually quite difficult and is rarely achieved successfully without guidance from an expert in the field of animal nutrition. Unless you *really* know what you're doing in terms of the science of feline nutrition, *exclusively* feeding your cat homemade meals is at best pure folly, and at worst downright dangerous for your cat.

Reputable pet food manufacturers budget substantial amounts of money for research to back claims that their products are nutritionally sound. Most have veterinary nutritionists and other specialists on staff, or they retain expert consultants. They also test their products in numerous ways to help ensure that they can uphold their guarantees. Without the guidance of a veterinarian or animal nutritionist who has been formally trained in feline nutrition, home-cooked feline diets lack this scientific basis and seldom contain adequate and balanced amounts of taurine and other essential nutrients to sustain good health in cats over a period of time.

Of course, this doesn't mean that you can never express your affection by cooking something special for your cat. Certainly, offering your cat an *occasional* homemade meal or a few table scraps now and then is OK, as long as you don't overdo it. But exclusively and routinely feeding a cat home-cooked meals should not be done, except in rare situations, such as when the animal is suspected of being allergic or sensitive to an additive or ingredient in commercially prepared foods. Even then, the ingredients and recipes of the home-cooked diet should be recommended and supervised by a veterinary nutritionist, and the cat's progress on the special diet should be closely monitored.

Also, when preparing home-cooked foods for your cat, remember to *thoroughly* cook all meats to kill any harmful bacteria or parasites. Here is a simple recipe that can be prepared from leftovers or shared with your cat during your own meals:

⅓ cup cooked brown rice
⅔ cup chopped and cooked (boiled or baked) chicken, boneless and skinless
1 tablespoon grated or chopped vegetables (excluding onion), cooked

Mix cooked ingredients and serve warm, but not hot. If your cat does not relish the rice and vegetables, omit these ingredients next time and simply serve the chopped, cooked chicken alone. However, it is important to remove all bones to reduce the chances of choking. Removing the skin reduces the fat intake. Do not serve chicken with breaded or fried toppings. Skinless and boneless cooked turkey may be substituted for chicken. *Because this recipe does not constitute a complete and balanced meal, it should be used only for occasional, complementary feeding.*

Discourage Begging Behaviors

The practice of feeding people food to cats often encourages them to beg, a habit that can become annoying and hard to break. If your cat never acquires a taste for people food in the first place, chances are it won't become a beggar, and you'll be able to eat your meals in peace. So a good way to avoid creating unwanted begging behavior is simply to stick with feeding cat food. However, when you do offer your cat table scraps or other people foods as an occasional treat, place the food in the cat's bowl. Never offer food directly from the table while you are eating, because this is a surefire way to create a persistent beggar.

Some cats allowed to sample table fare also will develop an appetite for unusual people foods. Owners have reported that their cats have craved everything from yogurt to pizza and from bread to brussels sprouts. Just because a cat likes some unusual food, however, doesn't mean that that food is good for it. While some occasional bread or vegetables may do no harm, avoid sweets, especially chocolates, which can be toxic to cats. Too much sugar is no better for your cat than it is for you. Keep an eye on your cat's waistline, and if tabby starts to look a little too tubby, eliminate the people foods and treats altogether.

Special Commercial Diets

When a cat develops a special problem that may be associated with diet, the owner's overwhelming temptation is often to quit feeding cat food and to start preparing homemade meals, in hopes of remedying the situation. As we have already discussed, routinely feeding a homemade diet is a bad idea for some very good reasons. It is also unnecessary labor, because, in most cases, scientifically formulated feline diets are available to safely manage many medical conditions, from obesity to kidney problems to lower urinary tract disorder. Because the pet food industry recognizes that many

cats have special dietary needs, a number of specialty pet food products proliferate the market. These range from the therapeutic diets dispensed by veterinarians to regular diets designed primarily for healthy cats, but that address specific consumer concerns, such as fat and calorie content, magnesium levels, or urinary pH balance. As always, if you suspect your cat has a weight condition or other problem that may require changes in feeding, consult a veterinarian first before switching to a different diet. The remainder of this chapter discusses certain situations that may require special diets. (Please refer also to the chapter Obesity: Making Fat Cats Fit, starting on page 86.)

Managing Feline Lower Urinary Tract Disorder

The urinary tract collects and disposes of urine through the bladder and a tube called the urethra. In female cats the urethra is short and wide, whereas in males this opening through which urine passes is longer and more narrow. For this reason, males are more prone to urinary tract blockages than females, although problems can occur in both sexes. In feline lower urinary tract disorder (FLUTD) (also called FUS for feline urologic syndrome), tiny mineral crystals form in the lower urinary tract and irritate the internal tissues. The best-known type of crystal to form in this manner is called *struvite.*

In response to the discomfort caused by the crystals, the cat may repeatedly lick its penis or vulva and urinate in unusual places, such as the bathtub. Feeling an uncomfortable urgency to urinate, the cat may make frequent trips to the litter box. The cat even may strain or cry as it attempts to void. Occasionally, people mistake this straining to urinate for constipation. If you notice these symptoms, or if you see blood in the urine, take your cat to a veterinarian immediately. If the crystals are large enough, they may block the urethra completely, creating a potentially life-threatening emergency. If the cat cannot eliminate its urine, the kidneys may sustain irreversible damage from the backup pressure. Within a short time, toxic wastes can build up in the blood with fatal consequences. With prompt medical treatment, most cats recover; however, recurrences are common. Often, bacterial infections in the bladder or urethra complicate matters. The veterinarian may prescribe medications and dietary changes to manage the condition.

Over the years, numerous dietary elements have been blamed in the formation of struvite crystals that can plug the urethra in FLUTD. The suspect list has included ash, magnesium, phosphorous, and calcium, among others. As each suspect ingredient was incriminated, major cat food manufacturers promptly reformulated their foods to reflect prevailing scientific and consumer concerns.

Current findings suggest that the overall mineral composition of cat food, rather than an excess of any single ingredient, determines whether the urine pH balance becomes too alkaline (too high), providing favorable conditions for crystals to form in the urinary tract. However, magnesium content remains a secondary concern, enough to warrant restricting dietary levels when managing FLUTD. This is because struvite crystals are composed of magnesium, ammonium, and phosphate, and it is believed that feeding lower levels of magnesium may help prevent FLUTD.

Reflecting this knowledge, specialty foods, designed to address this specific consumer concern and intended to help keep healthy cats healthy, proliferate the market bearing label claims of "low magnesium," "reduces urinary pH" or "helps maintain urinary tract health." Beyond these permissible statements, cat food manufacturers cannot claim that their general-market products treat or prevent FLUTD, or any disease, without review by the Food and Drug Administration, because to do so would be touting the diet as a drug. What makes these specialty diets able to live up to their stated claims is that they contain enough acidifying ingredients to help keep urine pH within moderately acidic ranges. But the same is also true of most regular commercial dry cat

For cats prone to urinary tract problems, a greater fluid intake helps promote better urine output. Always provide plenty of fresh, clean water.

foods now on the market. An acid urine helps dissolve the mineral crystals or prevents them from forming in the first place. Diets that promote a urine pH of 6.1 to 6.5 increase the solubility of struvite crystals and appear to reduce the risk of the disease.

A veterinarian may also dispense available diets that are scientifically formulated to manage chronic struvite-related FLUTD cases. Any product's represented claims in this regard should be supported by adequate research and testing. Because certain therapeutic diets may not be suitable for healthy cats, they must bear the statement "Use only as

directed by your veterinarian" on the label. For this reason, too, they are generally sold to the public by a veterinarian to help ensure that proper medical protocols are observed. Because not all cases of FLUTD are caused by struvite crystals, a veterinarian may first conduct appropriate diagnostic tests before dispensing a diet of this type.

Feeding urine-acidifying dry diets to cats on a free-choice basis also appears to be an important factor in maintaining an acid urine. This is due to a phenomenon called the *post-prandial alkaline tide*, or the alkaline urine that cats tend to develop after they eat a large meal.

Studies have shown that cats allowed to nibble throughout the day seem less inclined to experience the extremes of this alkaline tide. For this reason, the feeding guidelines on many dry cat foods that promote an acid urine may recommend offering the food in one of two ways: measure out the daily amount in a bowl and allow the cat to eat free-choice, or divide the amount into smaller meals offered at regular intervals throughout the day. Always allow the cat free access to plenty of fresh water, because a greater fluid intake helps promote better urine output and less concentrated urine.

With the increased use of magnesium-restricted and urine-acidifying commercial diets, researchers have also noted a decrease in struvite stones along with an increase in similar stones composed of calcium oxalate. This suggests that, even though studies clearly show that restricting magnesium and maintaining a slightly acidic urine may help prevent struvite-related urethral obstructions, specialty diets formulated for this purpose are not necessarily a cure-all for *all* cats, particularly if they have the potential to cause other problems. In fact, cats prone to develop calcium oxalate crystals should *not* be fed such diets, because the lower magnesium levels may aggravate the condition. In addition, kittens and breeding queens should not receive these diets. Nor should urine acidifying drugs be used con-

currently with any acidifying diet. While studies show that diets promoting moderate acidification are safe, potential side effects include depletion of potassium and taurine. For this reason, many commercial foods that contain acidifying ingredients (including the therapeutic diets) add extra amounts of potassium and taurine to the overall mix to help prevent such depletion.

Feeding Cats with Kidney Problems

Chronic renal failure is so common in cats that most animals that live long enough will develop it to some degree. While the disorder is sometimes seen in young cats, it is more likely to occur with advancing age. Once symptoms become apparent, the damage to the kidneys is irreversible, but it's possible to maintain the cat's comfort and well-being for months, even years, on a special diet designed to help ease the signs of renal problems.

The kidneys filter and remove waste products from the body. When they can no longer perform this function efficiently, the waste toxins begin to build up in the blood. Left unchecked, this condition can be fatal. Symptoms of decreasing kidney function include weight loss, increased urination, increased thirst, intermittent vomiting, and loss of appetite. A cat with kidney problems may also develop bad breath, mouth ulcers, and a noticeably dull hair coat. As the wastes build up in the blood, the cat feels distinctly unwell and may appear lethargic.

While medical treatment seeks to eliminate this waste buildup and restore the body's normal electrolyte balance, nutritional management is aimed at relieving the symptoms and improving the cat's quality of life. Special lower-protein, low-sodium, low-phosphorus therapeutic diets help accomplish this. Because malfunctioning kidneys are limited in their capacity to filter wastes that come primarily from dietary protein, restricting the protein levels in food helps minimize their workload, thereby easing the symptoms of the disease. As most diet-conscious people know, salt can increase fluid retention and blood pressure. That's why experts recommend lower sodium levels for cats suffering from chronic kidney disease. They also recommend lower phosphorus levels, because the compromised kidneys have lost their ability to efficiently excrete excess amounts of this mineral. This in turn upsets the delicately balanced calcium/phosphorus ratio. The end result can be bones that fracture easily. The diet also needs to have greater palatability and digestibility and more calories to ensure that the cat eats the food and doesn't continue to lose weight.

While restricted amounts of certain ingredients are essential in special diets for feline kidney problems, higher amounts of potassium and B-complex vitamins are needed. Because the increased urine output that accompanies kidney failure promotes the loss of these important nutrients in significant quantities, they must be added back into the diet at sufficient levels to avoid deficiencies.

Unlike many commercial cat foods that promote an acid urine to help prevent struvite-related lower urinary tract disorders, therapeutic diets for the management of chronic renal failure require a neutral urine pH. This is because cats with diseased kidneys can no longer efficiently regulate their body's acid-base balance. They are at risk of developing *metabolic acidosis*, an abnormal condition in which the blood and tissues become less alkaline than is safe. Understandably, adding more acid from cat foods that contain urine acidifiers would only exacerbate the problem.

Cat foods suitable for the management of chronic kidney failure are available through veterinarians. Obviously, this is because the diets are too restricted in protein and certain other nutrients to be fed safely to healthy cats. This also means they are not suitable for growing kittens or reproducing queens. It is also important to note that different kinds of renal disease exist, and a restricted protein diet may not be the best course of treatment in every case. Therefore, if you suspect your cat has kidney problems, consult a veterinarian for proper diagnosis and treatment.

Feeding the Convalescent Cat

As owners who have had to deal with the situation know, getting a sick cat to eat is easier said than done, especially if a change to a special diet is involved. The task can be particularly challenging if the cat's sense of smell, which drives its sense of taste, has been impaired by an upper respiratory infection. Always warm refrigerated food to body temperature before offering it to your cat. Also, offering a pungent food, such as canned tuna for cats, sometimes helps entice an unwell animal to eat, as does pouring tuna oil over the cat's regular food. In some cases, a veterinarian may dispense appetite stimulants or recommend force-feeding paste and liquid foods until the cat resumes its normal eating patterns. During illness and recovery, it is especially important to see that the cat continues to drink water so that dehydration from excessive fluid loss does not occur. If the cat refuses to drink, a veterinarian may have to administer liquids intravenously to restore fluids and maintain proper electrolyte balance.

Depending on your cat's condition and the length of convalescence, your veterinarian may dispense a special concentrated diet that is highly digestible and that provides more protein, amino acids, and energy than what your pet was eating prior to its illness, injury, or operation. This is because protein and amino acids are the major building blocks involved in the body's repair process. To effectively accomplish this intricate repair and recovery process, the body needs more energy from fats, proteins, and carbohydrates. Although concentrated diets are formulated to be especially tasty to better tempt convalescent cats to eat, getting them to consume the food can still be a challenge. The best approach is to offer the cat several small portions throughout the day. Because a special diet is formulated and intended for special needs, do not allow other pets in the household to eat it. Always feed a convalescing cat separately so you can tell exactly how much it has eaten.

Because sick cats like to seclude themselves, keep convalescing cats indoors, where you can keep a watchful eye on them.

Coping with Food Refusal

Loss of appetite in cats is nearly always an early warning signal that something is wrong. If the cat doesn't feel like eating, the problem could be medical, a sore throat, an upper respiratory congestion, an impacted hair ball, an abscessed tooth, kidney or liver failure, or one of several infectious diseases. The problem also could be an emotional or psychological reaction, triggered by the stress of moving to a new home, bringing a new pet into the household, or even leaving the cat at a boarding kennel. Sometimes a perfectly healthy cat will simply walk away from its food, perhaps because it doesn't like the smell or taste of a new brand or flavor. Whatever the cause, refusal of food for more than a few days can begin to seriously compromise a cat's health and should never be ignored. If the cat cannot be enticed to resume eating, a visit to the veterinarian is a must.

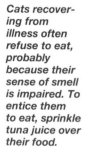

Cats recovering from illness often refuse to eat, probably because their sense of smell is impaired. To entice them to eat, sprinkle tuna juice over their food.

Hepatic Lipidosis

If a cat stops eating or begins to lose weight too rapidly, it can develop a potentially life-threatening liver condition called *hepatic lipidosis*, also known as fatty liver disease. While this condition is seen more frequently in obese cats that have been put on crash diets by their well-meaning owners, it can occur in any cat for reasons that often go unexplained. The disorder is caused by an excessive buildup of fat within the liver's cells. Treatment consists of getting the cat to eat and drink by whatever means necessary. Hospitalization may be required so the veterinarian can feed the cat intravenously through a tube. To avoid the serious consequences of this disease, don't delay in seeking medical advice for your cat when it goes off its feed. And *never* put a fat cat on a crash diet; always consult your veterinarian first to work out a safe and sensible weight-loss program. (Refer also to the chapter on Obesity: Making Fat Cats Fit, starting on page 86.)

Caring for Cats with Digestive Disorders

An array of disorders can create chronic digestive problems in cats

(see pages 103–111). Symptoms usually include vomiting and/or diarrhea and, depending on the cause and severity, a veterinarian may dispense a special diet to manage the disorder. Whether the diet is a short-term or a long-term solution, it will be highly digestible and likely will contain just enough soluble fiber to prolong the transit time of food through the gastrointestinal tract. The water-absorbing properties of dietary fiber can help control diarrhea, but too much can increase stool volume and have other adverse effects. Because fat absorption is often compromised when normal small intestine function is upset, a prescribed diet may also be moderately low in fat. While the cat is on the special diet, be sure to avoid offering snacks, food rewards, and table scraps, and follow your veterinarian's advice.

Coping with Food Allergies

Sometimes gastrointestinal upset with its accompanying vomiting and diarrhea may be symptomatic of an allergy. Like people, cats can be allergic to a host of things in their environment, including pollen, weeds, grasses, mold spores, house dust, feathers, wool, insect stings, drugs, chemicals, food ingredients, and even fleas. But instead of sneezing, watery eyes, and runny noses, cats' symptoms usually involve itchy

Suspect an itchy allergic reaction to flea bites if you notice your cat grooming itself excessively or biting at its skin.

skin, face, and ears. Typical warning signs include rubbing against furniture or carpet and excessive scratching, licking, or chewing at itchy places. Because skin irritation and scratching can also be caused by allergy to fleas, it's important to have your veterinarian distinguish the type of allergy and prescribe the best course of treatment.

Vomiting and diarrhea are more likely to occur if the *allergen,* or allergy-causing substance, is ingested in a food or drug. Redness, crusty skin, and hair loss around the nose, mouth, and face, while symptomatic of numerous other conditions, may also suggest a food allergy, or even an allergy to chemicals in plastic feeding dishes. In the latter case, replacing plastic dishes with lead-free ceramic or stainless steel ones is an easy remedy.

Unfortunately, most allergy cases are not so simple. Testing exists, but allergies remain difficult to diagnose. Treatment varies widely from patient to patient, depending on the cause and symptoms, and may include antihistamines or allergy shots. Recovery can take a long time. And because allergies usually persist for a lifetime, owners must commit to avoiding or reducing the allergen in the cat's environment for the rest of the animal's life.

In the case of a food allergy, treatment typically involves finding the offending ingredient and, if possible, eliminating it from the diet. Fortunately, food allergy is a relatively uncommon occurrence. When suspected, however, the offending ingredient is more likely to be a specific protein common to the foods the cat has been used to eating for awhile, rather than a recently introduced new brand or flavor of cat food. This is because the degree of exposure seems to be an important factor in the development of these types of allergies or sensitivities.

In such cases, the challenge is to eliminate the suspect foods and replace them with an adequate protein source that the cat has not been previously exposed to. Your veterinarian can suggest an appropriate diet, but recovery is usually a lengthy process of trial and error requiring a great deal of patience and owner compliance. Introducing new foods takes time and must be done gradually. During the test period, while you're trying to find and eliminate the offending ingredient, it's especially important to avoid feeding your cat table scraps or treats. You'll also need to stick with the special diet long enough to see results, which may take several months.

Although therapeutic diets are available for feeding allergic cats on a long-term basis, it's important to note that no truly *hypoallergenic* food for cats exists. This is because virtually any food ingredient can become an allergen, and it is impossible to predict what might cause an allergic reaction in any particular pet. While certain foods, such as lamb, chicken, and rice, have been touted as having less allergic potential than others, some cats develop sensitivities to these ingredients as well after being exposed to them for a period of time.

In cases where a cat does not do well on any prepared diet, the veterinarian may recommend specific recipes for home-cooked meals. These recipes will incorporate all necessary ingredients in the proper amounts, and to ensure complete and balanced nutrition they must be followed to the letter and closely supervised by a veterinarian. The cat's condition will need to be monitored regularly for signs of allergy or nutritional imbalances.

Feeding Cats with Heart Disease

Heart disease in the cat is often quite advanced by the time an owner notices and reports symptoms. There are several cardiac disorders that can affect the cat, but the most commonly known are cardiomyopathies, or diseases that affect the heart muscle. Different types of cardiomyopathies are classified according to the part of the heart affected. The problem can occur in cats of all ages, not just elderly cats. Symptoms may include lethargy, loss of appetite, difficulty breathing, sudden hind limb weakness, and fluid buildup in the chest or abdomen. The labored breathing is associated with fluid retention in the chest cavity in and around the lungs. The sudden hind limb weakness or paralysis is caused by blood clots that lodge in the blood vessels, usually in the pelvic region, blocking off sufficient circulation to that area. Often, this symptom is mistakenly believed to be the result of an accident.

One type of cardiomyopathy, called *dilated cardiomyopathy*, is caused by a deficiency of taurine in the diet. Fortunately, the disease is much less common than it used to be years ago, before this nutritional connection was established and before cat food manufacturers began adding more taurine to their food formulas.

Left untreated, cardiomyopathies progress to congestive heart failure and death, but with proper diet and medical management some afflicted cats can lead relatively normal lives. The available therapeutic low-sodium diets designed to manage such medical conditions help minimize fluid retention in the body, thus reducing the work load on the heart muscle. Along with a special diet, the veterinarian may dispense diuretic drugs that help remove excess fluid from the body. Because potassium, magnesium, and B-complex vitamins are readily lost during diuretic drug therapy, the special diet should also contain extra amounts of these nutrients to compensate.

Caring for Cats with Diabetes

Diabetes occurs primarily in overweight middle-aged or older cats. Symptoms may include increased urination, increased thirst, weight loss, lethargy, and poor coat condition. The disease is caused by the failure of the pancreas to produce adequate amounts of insulin. Insulin helps regulate the amount of sugar in the blood. Without enough insulin, sugar begins to build up in the blood. Left untreated, the condition can result in coma and death.

Treatment typically involves carefully monitored insulin therapy and dietary management. Success depends a great deal on the owner's adherence to a regular time schedule for administering both insulin and meals. Food portions must be consistent and offered at routine intervals to balance peak levels of blood sugar with appropriate insulin levels in the blood.

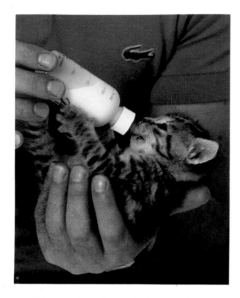

Often, the diet of choice for diabetic cats is one high in fiber ingredients that can help prolong the digestive process. These special diets are also generally reduced in fat. However, a variety of diets, including regular commercial ones, have been shown to work satisfactorily in many cases, as long as they are not high in simple sugars. More important than the type of diet is that the quantity fed and the time fed be as consistent as possible in conjunction with insulin therapy. If the cat is obese, an appropriate weight-reduction diet is a priority until normal weight is achieved. Likewise, if the cat has grown thin because of its illness, it may require an energy-dense food until it achieves the desired weight. Afterward, the veterinarian will need to reassess the cat's calorie needs and adjust the insulin therapy accordingly.

Hand-Fostering Orphaned Kittens

Ideally, the best way to handle motherless kittens is to find another nursing mother cat that will accept them and raise them as her own. You may get lucky by calling cat breeders or veterinarians and asking if they have a nursing queen on hand. If not, you'll have to choose between hand-fostering the kittens yourself or having them euthanized. Fostering orphaned or rejected kittens under six weeks old is a grueling task that requires feeding the little ones about every two hours around the clock, even throughout the night.

At each feeding, you also must massage the kittens' anuses and genitals with your finger or with a moist, warm cloth to stimulate urination and defecation. If you don't do this, the kittens will die, because they are too young to control their own bladder and bowel movements. Under normal circumstances, the mother cat tends to this chore herself by licking and cleaning the kittens' rear ends after each meal, which in turn stimulates the youngsters to void. At about three weeks of age, the kittens should begin urinating and defecating on their own, and you can start taking them to the litter box after meals.

To hand-foster kittens, you'll need to purchase a plastic nurser for kittens, preferably one that has a nipple similar in size and shape to a queen's teat. Or, failing to find such an item, an ordinary eyedropper will do. Between feedings, clean and sterilize the nurser or eyedropper in boiling water to kill harmful microorganisms. Feed a commercial kitten milk replacer, such as KMR, available through veterinarians and pet supply stores. Such formulas are specially made to serve as substitutes for queen's milk. Homogenized cow's milk is unsuitable for raising kittens because it doesn't contain enough protein, fat, and calories to meet their nutritional needs. Enriched, evaporated milk mixed half-and-half with warm water can be used *temporarily,* until you find an appropriate commercial feline formula. This mixture is also suitable for short-term use when kittens are transitioning to solid food, but don't rely on it as a staple food (see page 67).

Feed the amount recommended on the kitten formula package, although you may have to adjust this according to each kitten's individual needs. Before feeding, always warm the kitten formula to room temperature. Test it on your wrist before feeding to make sure it isn't too hot or too chilled.

Never hold a kitten on its back to feed. If you think about it, a kitten's natural nursing position is on its stomach, slightly inclined against its mother's belly. Therefore, this is how you should place the kitten to bottle-feed it. Tipping the kitten upward at a slight angle off a flat surface helps prevent air from entering the stom-

When hand-feeding a kitten, place the youngster on its stomach, never on its back.

ach as it feeds. Be careful not to force-feed a kitten, or it may accidentally aspirate liquid into its lungs. Let the kitten suckle the nipple and swallow at its own pace. If a kitten is too weak to suckle, consult a veterinarian, who can show you how to safely tube feed.

Kitten Development

Kittens weigh an average 3 or 4 ounces at birth, and within a week they should double their weight. To monitor the success of your hand-fostering efforts, weigh the kittens each day on a small food scale and record their progress. If one seems to be failing or lagging behind the others, consult a veterinarian. It's also important to keep newborn kittens warm by using a heating pad (on the lowest setting) or by placing the nesting box under an incandescent lightbulb. Leave one area of the nest unheated so that if a kitten gets too warm, it can move out of the way of the heat source.

In about ten days, the eyes begin to open. At first, all kittens' eyes are

By about 4 or 5 weeks of age, kittens can begin lapping milk from a bowl and experimenting with soft, solid food.

blue, changing to their adult shade at about 12 weeks of age. By 15 to 20 days old, kittens start crawling. Soon afterward, they begin to stand and toddle. By about four or five weeks, kittens can experiment with soft, solid foods, and weaning can begin (see page 67). Also by this time, they can control their own elimination, and litter box training can begin. Raising kittens in a confined area keeps them safe and also helps them toilet train faster.

Experts say that kittens handled frequently at an early age and socialized to humans grow up to be better-adjusted, people-oriented pets. But make sure the interaction is always gentle. Do not allow children to play with the kittens, as

their unintentional roughness can easily injure a young, fragile animal.

Dealing with Dental Problems

Often, an otherwise healthy cat that begins to slowly lose weight and condition will be found upon examination to have dental problems. Mouth ulcers and painful teeth or gums can cause a cat to refuse food, because it hurts too much to eat. While this problem can occur in all ages, it is seen more frequently in older cats. Often, the only noticeable symptoms are weight loss or a decline in eating. If your cat appears to have difficulty eating, look inside the mouth for clues. An adult cat has 30 permanent teeth, which should be white with little or no discoloration. Healthy gums are pink; diseased gums are tender, red, and swollen. A cat with dental disease often has bad breath, and if its teeth are sore it may flinch when you try to stroke the side of its face.

Untreated dental disease allows bacteria to leak into the bloodstream from sore, infected gums, compromising your cat's immune system and overall health. Brownish plaque and tartar buildup on the teeth can cause *gingivitis,* a chronic inflammation of the gums. Gradually, the gums recede and the teeth loosen. Painful abscesses may form in pockets around the loose teeth. The best way to prevent such discomfort is to regularly brush or rinse your cat's teeth with oral hygiene products designed for use in animals. Ask your veterinarian to demonstrate these products for you when he or she examines your cat's teeth at its next annual checkup. From time to time, your cat's oral health may benefit from a professional cleaning. For this procedure the cat is anesthetized, and the veterinarian uses an ultrasonic scaler to blast away the ugly, brown tartar and polish the teeth.

A cat recovering from dental surgery may need a soft diet of canned food for several days before resuming dry rations. Cats that have lost their canines and the tiny teeth in front can still chew dry rations

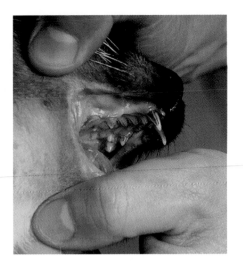

Plaque and tartar buildup eventually lead to sore teeth and inflamed gums, which can cause a cat to stop eating and lose weight and body condition.

adequately, but loss of the molars and incisors may necessitate a soft diet of canned food or moistened dry kibble.

Toothbrushing

Cats can be hard cases, but not impossible, to accustom to having their mouths gently opened and handled. The key is to start early,

Bad teeth and inflamed gums (gingivitis) can make your cat's mouth too sore to eat properly. Toothbrushing two or three times a week and dental checkups can help prevent plaque and tartar buildup.

process without much fuss. If the cat struggles, don't force it to submit. Doing so will only make it resist you harder. Instead, be extra gentle and patient so it won't learn to dread having its mouth handled. Praise your cat afterward.

Feeding Your Cat When Traveling or Boarding

When traveling with your cat, take along its bed, a favorite toy, feeding bowls, food, and any medications required. These familiar objects will help provide the cat with a sense of security in strange surroundings. It's also a good idea to pack a gallon or two of water from home, in case the cat refuses to drink the different-tasting water in the new place. Because cats are creatures of habit, adhere to your regular feeding schedule as closely as possible. Just in case the travel jitters cause your cat to go off its feed, take along a can or two of tuna-flavored cat food. The strong odor of tuna is often sufficient to entice most finicky felines to resume eating.

Before boarding your cat, ask what type of food it will receive. If you have any doubts as to whether your cat will eat the standard fare offered, provide your own. Likewise, if your cat requires a special or therapeutic diet of any kind, supply the boarding facility with

while your cat is still a kitten. Older cats take a longer time to train and may never completely accept the idea of having their teeth brushed. You will need a small pet toothbrush with ultra-soft bristles or one designed to fit over your fingertip for easier use. In addition, purchase a nonfoaming, enzymatic toothpaste made especially for cats. These pastes, designed to dissolve plaque without a lot of scrubbing action, come in fish, poultry, and malt flavors for finicky felines. *Never* use human toothpaste on a cat because it can burn the back of the throat.

To begin training, dip your finger in something tasty, such as canned cat food juice, and gently rub the cat's teeth and gums. After about a week of this, try using the toothbrush on only a few teeth on one side of the mouth. If your cat doesn't accept the brush right away, wrap gauze around your finger and gently massage the teeth and gums. With each try, clean a few more teeth, until your cat gradually accepts the

enough rations from home to last the duration of your absence. Leave any special feeding instructions in writing with the facility's operator, along with where you can be reached and which veterinarian to call in case of an emergency.

Odd and Not-So-Odd Eating Behaviors

Pica is an abnormal craving for and frequent ingestion of unnatural or nonnutritional substances, such as dirt, feces, newspaper, or litter box filler. Fortunately, the condition is not as common in cats as *coprophagia,* or dung-eating, is in the dog. While exploring kittens often attempt to experimentally taste new things upon first exposure, it is considered abnormal for an adult cat to eat or crave inedible materials. Such behavior warrants investigation by a veterinarian and may be attributed to a dietary imbalance or a nervous system disorder.

Wool and fabric chewing: This neurotic behavior is thought to stem more from emotional rather than dietary causes, although experts believe a craving for fiber or roughage may play a contributory role. Certain breeds, such as the Siamese, seem more prone to the behavior than others. While knitted wools seem to be the preferred target, afflicted cats will chew gaping holes in any available fabric—

For safe traveling with your cat, always transport it in a sturdy pet carrier.

socks, sweaters, blankets, drapes, bedspreads, even furniture upholstery. Some cats will also show an odd preference for licking or chewing vinyl shower curtains or plastic table cloths, perhaps because of a thin, oily coating of fat that helps make certain materials pliable and waterproof. Certainly, this behavior is potentially dangerous and must be dealt with quickly and systematically, as the consumed materials can lead to deadly intestinal obstructions (see page 110).

While dog owners expect and prepare for their puppies to go through a destructive chewing phase, cat owners are typically surprised and bewildered by such behavior in their feline companions. Fortunately, the behavior is not all that common in the cat. But once established as a habit, destructive chewing can be quite difficult to halt.

not always, regurgitated along with some hair.

The problem with grass-eating felines is that they often extend their fondness for greenery to decorative indoor house plants. This can be particularly hazardous, as numerous plants are toxic to cats (see page 139). Naturally, cats cannot tell the difference between a poisonous plant and a nonpoisonous one. Therefore, the owner needs to make the house cat-safe by replacing potentially dangerous plants with harmless varieties. Then, to discourage the cat from snacking on safe decorative plants, place them out of reach or give the cat its own plant to help satisfy its craving. Pet stores sell grass kits for growing your kitty's own personal veggie stand. To help the cat learn to discriminate between plants it can and cannot eat, place the special stand of kitty grass near the cat's food bowl, but well away from the other house plants. If you catch the cat in the act of eating one of your favorite house plants, startle the animal by yelling "No!" loudly; or squirt the cat with clean jets of water from a water pistol. Never hit the cat with your hand or with any object, as this will only make it fear humans. While the startle method works well for training most cats, some will continue to sneak a few bites of forbidden greenery when the owner is not present. This is why it's important to make sure all accessible plants in your house are nontoxic to cats.

Being naturally curious, cats sometimes lick or chew on things they shouldn't. To make your home cat-safe, do the same things you would do to make it child-safe.

Owners and veterinarians alike often recommend applying a nontoxic but unpleasant-tasting substance to fabrics as a temporary deterrent. The strategy is to use a repellent as often as necessary until the cat develops an unfavorable association with the material. Recommended repellents include Tabasco sauce, hot pepper sauce, raw onion juice, and bitter lime or bitter apple (available in spray bottles at pet stores). Ultimately, the best tactic may be simply to remove the fabrics the cat has been eating, or restrict the cat's access to the area where the materials are.

Eating grass and house plants:
Eating grass is a perfectly normal behavior for cats, although a happily grazing feline may seem odd to the uninitiated cat owner. Although the exact reason why cats eat greenery is not known, grass is thought to be a natural purgative and may help clear the system of excess swallowed hair. In fact, grass is often, but

Chapter 10
Things Your Cat Should NOT Consume

While some people mistakenly assume that animals can instinctively recognize harm and avoid poisonous substances in and around the home, nothing could be further from the truth. Cats, like children, don't always know what's good for them or what's bad. Occasionally, their curiosity leads to the unwitting ingestion of an inedible object or a toxic and potentially fatal substance. Following is a general discussion of some of the most common potentially harmful items or toxic substances found in and around the home and how you can make your house cat-safe.

Flea Control Products

Appropriate flea control measures are a must for ridding your cat of these pesky parasites; however, indiscriminate use and inappropriate mixing of incompatible products can result in toxic, even fatal, consequences. For example, using certain sprays, powders, or medicated shampoos in conjunction with a flea collar or an oral flea control medicine may be unsafe as well as unnecessary. Likewise, sprays or other products used to treat the cat's bedding or the environment may not be appropriate when used *on* the pet or in combination with certain on-pet preparations. Your veterinarian can tell you which products can be used together safely and effectively for controlling fleas on the pet and in its environment.

The first rule to follow when selecting products is: *Always read the label before applying any product to your cat.* The second rule is: *Choose only products that are labeled as safe for use on cats.* Never use flea control products or shampoos on cats that are formulated solely for dogs. Certain products that are safe for dogs may be harmful or even fatal to cats, because the medications and insecticides are too concentrated or simply incompatible with the feline physical makeup. Likewise, many flea control products

If you allow your cat to go outside unsupervised, it risks encounters with many outdoor hazards, from accidental exposure to pesticides and other chemicals to eating contaminated or poisoned food and garbage.

that are safe for use on adult cats may not be safe for use on kittens, especially those under six weeks of age. Similarly, some products may not be suitable for use on pregnant cats. Also, some products can be used to control fleas safely in the pet's quarters or on its bedding but not directly on the pet's fur. So read labels carefully and follow the directions before using any flea control product on your cat or in its living environment. Then, if you still have doubts or questions about using a certain product, call your veterinarian's office for advice.

Before treating an indoor area for fleas or activating flea foggers in the home, remove cats and other animals from the rooms. Cover or remove all foodstuffs, as well as food and water dishes, so they will

not be contaminated by the spray residue. Thoroughly air out the area, according to the label directions, before allowing animals to reenter.

Reactions to Flea Control Products

Be aware that certain flea products can cause some cats to salivate a little immediately after application. In many cases, this is no cause for concern, and the reaction usually subsides after a minute or two. However, if the reaction doesn't subside quickly, be prepared to take action. If the cat begins salivating *heavily* after you've applied a topical flea preparation to its fur, or if the cat staggers or shows obvious signs of distress, rinse the substance off *immediately* with warm water and call your veterinarian for further advice. It may be necessary to transport the animal to a clinic for medical treatment.

If your cat experiences a reaction to any product, it is best to discontinue using it and ask your veterinarian to recommend an alternative. There are numerous other products on the market that your veterinarian can suggest for safe, effective flea control.

Antifreeze

The pleasant taste of traditional antifreeze attracts many animals to drink from roadside or driveway puddles, but as little as half a teaspoon can be lethal to an adult cat. *Ethylene glycol* is the active ingredient in conventional antifreeze that is highly poisonous to animals and children. Preventing your cat's exposure to this deadly substance is just one more good reason to keep your cat companion safely indoors at all times. However, to make your garage and driveway safer for all other pets and wildlife in the neighborhood, always hose down and clean up fluid leaks and antifreeze spills immediately. When adding antifreeze to your car's radiator or overflow tank, use a funnel to avoid spillage and wipe up any stray drops that miss their mark.

Safer Antifreeze Products

When it comes time to flush out your car's cooling system, consider replacing your traditional antifreeze

As little as one-half teaspoon of traditional antifreeze can kill a full-grown cat.

with one of several safer antifreeze brands now on the market. Ask your automotive technician to recommend one. These safer antifreeze products contain *propylene glycol*, which is significantly less toxic than the ethylene glycol in conventional brands. In fact, propylene glycol is FDA-approved for use in some foods, alcoholic beverages, cosmetics, and pharmaceuticals.

Although not without potential problems, propylene glycol is considered to be about three times safer, if not more so, than the ethylene glycol contained in conventional antifreeze products. This means that a cat who licks a small spill on the garage floor can ingest about three times more of a safer antifreeze brand without suffering the devastating effects of conventional antifreeze. Still, it's feasible for an animal to consume enough propylene glycol to become sick, and if a large enough dose is ingested coma or death can result. The dosage truly determines the extent of the poisoning. When ingested in small amounts, propylene glycol is metabolized into lactic acids. These are normal body constituents that do little harm. But in unusual amounts, the presence of these acids may lead to certain imbalances that require medical treatment. However, unlike ethylene glycol, the prognosis for an animal poisoned by propylene glycol is much better, due to the lack of renal involvement and subsequent kidney damage. In the early stages, propylene glycol's effects are similar to that of the deadlier antifreeze types, producing symptoms of central nervous system depression and marked sleepiness in the afflicted animal.

Ethylene glycol in conventional antifreeze kills by causing acute kidney failure. Often, by the time the owner notices something is wrong and seeks veterinary assistance, the damage is usually too far progressed to be undone, and the prognosis for recovery is poor. Depending on the amount ingested, death from conventional antifreeze poison-ing can come quickly in a matter of four to five hours, or it may drag on for several agonizing days. During the first 12 hours after ingestion, central nervous depression sets in. The animal acts tired and sleeps more than normal and may even stagger and appear drunk. About 24 hours after ingestion, the animal enters the renal stage, and once the situation has progressed this far the chance of survival is not good. At this point, the options may include fluid therapy, dialysis, or euthanasia. While kidney transplants have been performed on cats, this treatment method is expensive, not readily available in most areas, and still quite experimental.

Aspirin and Acetaminophen

Ingredients in common, over-the-counter painkillers for humans can be deadly to cats, especially *acetaminophen,* the active agent in Tylenol. In addition, medications containing aspirin, ibuprofen, and naproxen sodium are potentially deadly to cats. Unlike people, cats cannot effectively metabolize the ingredients in these drugs in their livers, and the result can be liver failure.

Unfortunately, a number of poisonings occur annually because some people mistakenly assume that, because aspirin and similar drugs are so safe for humans, they must be OK for cats. Such an unin-

Cat's don't have to drink poisons to get sick. They can walk through spills or brush against dirty containers, then lick the substance off their fur and paws.

formed assumption can have deadly consequences, because aspirin, acetaminophen, and ibuprofen are definitely *not* safe for cats. Even small amounts, or just one tablet, can cause depression, vomiting, diarrhea, and death in cats.

In certain cases, a medical professional may effectively prescribe aspirin to treat a cat's condition, but the dosage is *very* low and must be carefully controlled to avoid toxic side effects or a fatal overdose. While there are some drugs designed for humans that can be given safely to cats, *never* attempt to administer any human medication, including aspirin, to your cat without the supervision of a veterinarian. To avoid accidental poisoning, keep aspirin, Tylenol, and all other medications, including vitamin and mineral supplements, whether prescription or over-the-counter, tightly capped and stored safely behind closed doors in the medicine cabinet, just as you would do if you have small children in the house. Never leave pills lying exposed on countertops, where a cat might discover them. Likewise, leaving out opened or loosely capped vitamin bottles or other medicines is an invitation to disaster, as an exploring cat may knock them over, spill the contents, and perhaps accidentally consume one or more pills or tablets in the spirit of play, while batting them about the floor. Also, if you drop a pill on the floor, make sure you find it and discard it before allowing your cat access to that area. Most cough syrups contain alcohol, which is hazardous to cats even in small amounts, so keep these containers tightly closed and out of reach as well.

Holiday Hazards

Aspirin can even be a potential hazard at Christmas time, because it is frequently used as a preservative in Christmas tree water to prevent live trees from drying out so quickly. Commercial chemical preservatives may be used for this purpose as well, but these or aspirin in the water can make a lethal cocktail for cats that lap water from the Christmas tree base. Avoid using these chemicals, keep cats out of the decorated room, or put up an artificial tree that requires no watering.

The holidays can pose many other hazards for cats as well, because of all the enticing tinsel and decorations

Tinsel poses a potential holiday hazard for kitties who love to play with the dangling strands. If swallowed, garland, tinsel, and gift wrapping ribbon can cause a serious intestinal blockage that may require surgery.

draped over tree branches, banisters, and fireplaces. Cats especially love to play with and eat the garland and tinsel that dangles so alluringly from the Christmas tree. While not toxic, the string-like foil material can cause serious intestinal obstructions when swallowed. The same is true of angel hair, edible ornaments, and small plastic beads or berries. In addition, many people decorate with poinsettia, holly berries, and mistletoe, all of which can be toxic to cats if eaten. Avoid using these types of decorations, or restrict the cat's access to decorated rooms. Keep the lower branches of the Christmas tree free of ingestible or breakable items.

Alcohol

During holiday parties or other special occasions, pick up unattended alcoholic beverages immediately so your cat won't be tempted to sample the spirits. Better yet, stow your cat safely away in a quiet, undisturbed area of the house while you are entertaining guests. This way, no one will be tempted to offer it "treats" that aren't good for it. Unfortunately, some people think it's funny to see a cat lap a few sips of beer or liquor, then watch it stagger in drunken circles. But alcohol is toxic to cats, even in small amounts, so never let anyone offer your cat a "spiked" drink. This practice is cruel and dangerous, because a cat's smaller body mass cannot adequately absorb alcohol's toxic effects. Just a little "hair of the dog" can turn deadly and fatally affect an animal's breathing.

Chocolate

While a favorite treat for many humans, chocolate can be toxic to cats, so never offer these sweets to your pet for reward or affection. Also, avoid leaving desserts and candy dishes exposed where your cat might sample the goodies when you're not looking. The offending ingredient in chocolate is called *theobromine,* which occurs in differing concentrations in different kinds of chocolate. For example, milk chocolate, the kind used in most candy bars, is not quite as lethal because it is diluted by the other ingredients, milk, sugar, and so on, and a larger quantity is generally required to produce the toxic side effects. Baking chocolate, however, contains theobromine in more concentrated amounts; therefore, consuming a lesser amount can be lethal. To be safe, consider *any* amount of any kind of chocolate

Alcohol is dangerous for cats. When entertaining, keep an eye out for unattended or leftover drinks and discard them so your cat won't be tempted to sample the goods.

dangerous for a cat to ingest and take the appropriate steps to prevent your cat's exposure to it.

Household Chemicals

Cats don't have to directly eat or drink poisonous substances to get sick. Being the fastidiously clean creatures they are, they often fall victim to poisonings simply because of their clean habits. They can accidentally ingest wax, bleach, household insecticides, detergents, and other toxic chemicals simply by brushing against dirty containers, walking through spills, or padding across freshly waxed floors, then licking the foreign substance off their paws or fur. They can also inhale or ingest poisons, the same way people can. With these facts in mind, take an inventory of all household chemicals and other potential hazards in your home that a climbing, exploring cat might have access to. Then, to make your home cat-safe, do the same things you would do to make it child-safe. Store detergents, solvents, mothballs, insect sprays, and all other household chemicals out of reach in securely closed cabinets. Put tight-fitting lids on all trash bins so that foraging cats won't get sickened by spoiled foodstuffs or injured by discarded razor blades, broken glass, or jagged tin can edges. Remove poisonous plants from the cat's immediate environment. Avoid using edible rodent and insect baits

in areas where your cat might get at them and get poisoned. Keep perfumes, cosmetics, and nail polish removers tightly capped and out of reach. Also, if you use chemicals in the toilet bowl or tank for ongoing cleaning and disinfection, keep the toilet lid *down* to prevent cats from drinking the bowl water. Accidental ingestion may also occur if the cat falls into an open toilet, but scrambles out, only to lick the chemically tainted water from its wet fur.

Don't bathe your cat with dish washing liquids or human shampoos without first consulting your veterinarian. Certain products may be safe for this purpose, while others aren't, but why risk letting your cat be the guinea pig? Do some research and ask some questions first. Also, avoid using bleach and other common household disinfectants for cleaning cat bowls, litter pans, living quarters, or bedding. Some of these products contain ingredients, such as *phenols,* that are toxic to cats if, for example, ingested from an accidental spill. Also, most animals are turned off by the odor of bleach and other strong-smelling chemicals, especially in their litter pans, and some may even refuse to use the same box again. Instead, use hot water to disinfect cat boxes. Use a mild, unscented dish soap for washing food and water bowls, and make sure all residue is rinsed away. Select stainless steel or lead-free ceramic bowls so they can be sterilized in the dishwasher. Plastic ones can melt or warp if not dishwasher safe. For mopping and cleaning a pet's quarters, shop at your pet store for disinfecting and odor-neutralizing products designed specifically for safe use in kennels and catteries.

When hiring a professional exterminator, stipulate that the products used in your home must be safe for pets. Find out the name of the chemicals to be used, then check with your veterinarian about the precautions you need to take to protect your pet. In some cases, pets and people have to vacate the premises for a period of time, and it may even be necessary to board the animal away from home for a night or two. Whether you use professional services or over-the-counter flea foggers, always make sure treated areas have been properly aired out, as directed on the product label, before reentering.

To deter your cat from nibbling on your house plants, purchase a "kitty grass" kit from a pet shop and grow a special patch of greens just for your cat.

Lawn and Garden Chemicals

Never use any household or lawn and garden pesticide on a cat or on its bedding for the control of fleas, ticks, or other external parasites, unless the label specifically states that it is safe and intended for use on cats or pet bedding. Many fertilizers, herbicides, and other lawn treatments can be potentially hazardous to pets that walk across freshly treated areas, then lick the substance from their paws. The compounds in some fertilizers will even burn cats' paws if they happen to tramp across a fresh application. Read labels before applying these chemicals around your home and yard. If you use a lawn service, ask about the potential hazards to domestic animals with each product application. In some cases, it may be necessary to confine your cat indoors until the first rain washes the fertilizer or lawn treatment into the soil. Also, ask your neighbors to inform you before they spray or treat their lawns so you can arrange to keep your pet safely indoors.

Hazardous Plants

Although carnivorous by nature, cats enjoy snacking on greenery, apparently because the added roughage aids in digestion. Unfortunately, cats often indulge this occasional craving by nibbling on decorative house plants and ornamental shrubs. While many plants are harmless to cats, others are deadly. Ingestion can cause a wide range of symptoms, including mouth irritation, drooling, vomiting, diarrhea, hallucinations, convulsions, lethargy, coma, and death. If your cat displays any unusual behavior after chewing on a plant, consult a veterinarian immediately, or call the National Animal Poison Control Information Center (see p. 140).

Plants that can produce symptoms of illness or irritation, whether mild or severe, are considered toxic and should be removed from the cat's environment. To make your house and yard cat-safe, avoid keeping the common toxic plants listed below.

This list is only a partial one; therefore, if you are unsure about a particular plant's toxicity, call your veterinarian. The National Animal Poison Control Information Center also offers a comprehensive list of plants toxic to cats.

First Aid for Accidental Poisoning

If you suspect your cat has ingested a potentially hazardous substance, contact your veterinarian immediately. Similarly, if your cat's coat or paws become contaminated by bleach, pesticides, paint products, household cleaners and disinfectants, oil, tar, antifreeze, or other potential poisons, wash off the offending substance immediately. If

Hazardous Plants

Amaryllis	Daffodil	Ivy	Oleander
Asparagus Fern	Daphne	Jack-in-the-	Periwinkle
Azalea	Datura	Pulpit	Peyote
Belladonna	Delphinium	Jerusalem Cherry	Philodendron
Bird of Paradise	Dieffenbachia	Jimsonweed	Poinsettia
Black Locust	(Spotted	Larkspur	Pokeweed
Caladium	Dumb Cane)	Lily of the Valley	Potato
Castor Bean	Elephant Ear	Lupin	Rhododendron
Chinaberry	Foxglove	Marijuana	Rhubarb
Christmas	Fruit Pits	Mistletoe	Skunk Cabbage
Cherry	Hemlock	Monkshood	Spider Mum
Christmas Rose	Henbane	Moonseed	Tobacco
Chrysanthemum	Holly	Morning Glory	Umbrella Plant
Clematis	Honeysuckle	Mushrooms	Wild Cherry
Creeping Charlie	Hydrangea	Nightshade	Wisteria
Crown of Thorns	Iris	Nutmeg	Yew

If your cat's natural fondness for munching on greens extends to your house plants, be aware that many common varieties are poisonous or irritating to felines.

necessary, clip away the affected fur. If the coat appears to be heavily saturated, or if you believe the cat may have already licked some of the substance from its coat or paws, seek veterinary advice right away.

Do not attempt to induce vomiting unless an expert advises you to do so. Some caustic substances do twice as much damage when vomited back up. If, after describing the situation to your veterinarian or poison control center via telephone, you are instructed to induce vomiting, do so as directed. Often, this will involve administering a liquid emetic, such as a small amount of syrup of ipecac or hydrogen peroxide, by mouth with an eyedropper. Syrup of ipecac is a common, over-the-counter emetic that is usually readily available in most household medicine cabinets. In fact, it's good to keep on hand for such emergencies. Hydrogen peroxide is a common household antiseptic; however,

it is useless if it no longer bubbles. If you don't have either of these handy, warm salt water sometimes works. To administer a liquid emetic, tilt the cat's head back slightly, insert an eyedropper or syringe (without the needle) into the corner of the mouth and gently squirt in a few drops at a time. Do not squirt the medication into the cat's mouth too quickly or too forcefully, as this may cause the cat to accidentally inhale the liquid, which can lead to pneumonia. Hold the mouth shut and stroke the cat's throat until it swallows.

If you know or suspect the identity of the poisonous substance the cat has ingested, take a small sample or the entire package, as applicable, with you to the veterinary clinic. Or, if the cat has vomited, scoop up a small sample in a plastic bag so the veterinarian can analyze the contents. This will help the veterinarian determine the best antidote to administer or the best method of treatment.

National Animal Poison Control Information Center

For 24-hour assistance, seven days a week, call the National Animal Poison Control Information Center, operated by the University of Illinois College of Veterinary Medicine. The hotline number is (800) 548-2423. The service charges a fee for each initial case, payable by credit card. Or you may have the charge added to your telephone bill by calling (900) 680-0000.

Transporting an Ill or Poisoned Cat

A cat that is unconscious or obviously in distress must receive immediate medical attention. Delaying transport to an animal clinic may mean the difference between life and death. If the cat is struggling, anxious, or convulsing, wrap it in a towel or blanket, leaving only the head sticking out. Remember, no matter how gentle your cat, it may bite or claw you if it's frightened or in pain. Transport the cat in a pet carrier if you have one. Position an unconscious cat on its side for transport and cover it with a blanket to keep it warm. If the cat is lying down, approach it from behind, slide one hand under the chest and one hand under the rump, and gently place it in a pet carrier or on a blanket for transport. If the cat is crouched, grasp the scruff of the neck with one hand, place the other hand under the hips and rear legs for support, and cradle the cat in your arms.

Be Observant and Prepared

Cats often conceal illness or pain, but observant owners can detect subtle behavior changes that reveal all is not well. Because early detection can greatly improve treatment possibilities and the odds of a full recovery, it is important to observe and know your cat's feeding habits and daily routines. If you notice anything out of the ordinary, keep the cat confined until you can transport it to a veterinarian. If you let a sick, injured, or poisoned cat go outdoors, it may seek solace in some hideaway. Then, by the time you find the animal, *if* you find it, it may be too late to render effective treatment.

To successfully cope with any emergency, be prepared, stay calm, and act quickly. Keep your veterinarian's emergency telephone number handy, taped to the refrigerator or in some other visible place. When an emergency arises, call ahead to your veterinary clinic, or ask someone else to, if possible, before transporting your pet. This way, the hospital staff can prepare for your arrival and, depending on the situation, tell you what first aid measures to use en route. Remember, responsible pet owners who take the time to be observant and prepared and who make the effort to educate themselves about proper cat care and nutrition can contribute significantly to their pets living longer and healthier lives.

Feline Body Condition*

❶ **EMACIATED** Ribs visible on shorthaired cats; no palpable fat; severe abdominal tuck; lumbar vertebrae and wing of ilia easily palpated.

❷ **VERY THIN** Shared characteristics of body conditions 1 and 3.

❸ **THIN** Ribs easily palpable with minimal fat covering; lumbar vertebrae obvious; obvious waist behind ribs; minimal abdominal fat.

❹ **UNDERWEIGHT** Shared characteristics of body conditions 3 and 5.

❺ **IDEAL** Well proportioned; observe waist behind ribs; ribs palpable with slight fat covering; abdominal fat pad minimal.

❻ **OVERWEIGHT** Shared characteristics of body conditions 5 and 7.

❼ **HEAVY** Ribs not easily palpated with moderate fat covering; waist poorly discernable; obvious rounding of abdomen; moderate abdominal fat pad.

❽ **OBESE** Shared characteristics of body conditions 7 and 9.

❾ **GROSSLY OBESE** Ribs not palpable under heavy fat cover; heavy fat deposits over lumbar area, face, and limbs; distention of abdomen with no waist; extensive abdominal fat deposits.

*Adapted with permission from the Ralston Purina Company, St. Louis, Missouri.

Glossary

AAFCO The Association of American Feed Control Officials, an agency that proposes and develops regulations related to the production and labeling of animal feeds.

Abyssinian One of the oldest known breeds of cat characterized by its slender, athletic build and its ticked or "agouti" coat pattern.

Ad libitum Common term used when referring to free-choice or at-will feeding methods.

Adulterated Containing potentially harmful substances or contaminants.

Alkaline In referring to urine, having a high pH of 7.0 or more.

Allergen A substance or ingredient that can cause an allergic reaction.

Alter To spay or neuter (verb); a cat that has been spayed or neutered (noun).

Amino acids The chief components or building blocks of proteins that are synthesized by living cells or derived from the diet.

Anemia A medical condition characterized by a low red blood cell count.

Anorexia Lack of appetite.

Antibodies Important elements of the immune system response that help the body defend itself against disease.

Antioxidants Substances in certain foods that function at the cellular level to help protect the body against cell damage from free radicals.

Ascorbic acid Vitamin C.

Avidin An enzyme in raw egg white that renders *biotin*, an important B-complex vitamin, useless and unavailable in the cat's body.

Bacteria Microscopic organisms that, depending on the type, can cause disease or stimulate chemical reactions important to nutrition.

Beta-carotene Vitamin A derived from plant sources.

Bile A substance produced by the liver that is important in the proper absorption of fats.

Butylated hydroxyanisole (BHA) and **butylated hydroxytoluene (BHT)** Chemical preservatives added to some pet foods to prevent fat rancidity.

Byproducts In referring to pet foods, the animal parts and cuts of meat derived from the human food industry that are not generally used for human consumption, such as the heart, brain, tongue, stomach, etc.

Calorie The amount of heat needed to raise the temperature of a gram of water by 1°C.

Cardiomyopathy A disease of the heart muscle; one type, called *dilated cardiomyopathy*, has been linked with a deficiency of taurine in the diet.

Carnivorous Meat-eating; dependent on the consumption of animal protein for health and well-being.

Cat fancy A collective term generally applied to those who have a serious interest in breeding and showing purebred cats.

Cholecalciferol A form of Vitamin D.

Colitis Inflammation of the colon or large intestine.

Colostrum The first milk secreted after birth, which contains high levels of antibodies.

Cyanocobalamin Vitamin B12.

Dehydration Loss of body fluids.

Digestibility An assessment of the amount of protein present in a food that can actually be absorbed and used by the animal that consumes it.

Digests Liquefied or powdered fats and animal tissues sprayed on dry foods to enhance flavor and palatability.

Domestication Adaption to life with humans.

Eclampsia A medical condition caused by calcium deficiency in the lactating queen; milk fever.

Enteritis Irritation or inflammation of the small intestine.

Epiglottis A tissue flap in the back of the mouth that automatically closes over the windpipe during swallowing to prevent food from entering the lungs.

Esophagus The muscular tube that carries food from the mouth to the stomach.

Estrus The recurrent cycles of being "in heat," during which time an intact female cat of reproductive age is receptive to the male and will mate.

Ethoxyquin An antioxidant used as a preservative in some pet foods to prevent fat rancidity.

Euthanasia The act of painlessly ending an animal's life for humane reasons.

Exotic Shorthair A recognized breed of cat often described as a shorthaired Persian and characterized by its rounded head, flat face, and short, cobby body.

Extrusion The process of manufacturing dry cat foods by rapidly cooking raw materials at a high temperature in a large cylindrical channel called an "extruder."

Feces The product of bowel movements.

Feline immunodeficiency virus (FIV) A viral infection that attacks a cat's immune system; also called feline AIDS, for which no approved vaccine is yet available.

Feline infectious peritonitis (FIP) An often fatal infection in cats caused by a coronavirus that progresses in one of two forms, "wet" or "dry." A preventive vaccine is available.

Feline leukemia virus (FeLV) The most common infectious disease complex of domestic cats today, caused by a retrovirus and often resulting in a range of symptoms and related disorders; can be prevented by annual vaccination.

Feline panleukopenia virus (FPV) A highly contagious disease of cats caused by a parvovirus, which can be prevented by annual vaccination; also called feline distemper or feline enteritis.

Feline urologic syndrome (FUS) Also called "feline lower urinary tract disease" or FLUTD, this potentially life-threatening medical condition is caused by tiny mineral crystals that form in the urinary tract, leading to painful irritation or serious blockages.

Feral Wild or undomesticated.

Free radicals Unstable oxygen molecules, produced during normal body metabolism, that can steal electrons from stable molecules, triggering potentially detrimental chemical changes inside the body called "oxidation."

Gingivitis A dental disorder characterized by inflammation of the gums.

Hepatic lipidosis A potentially life-threatening medical condition characterized by an excessive buildup of fat in the liver; also called fatty liver disease.

Heredity Inheritance, or the sum of qualities transmitted genetically from parent to offspring.

Hormone A natural chemical secreted by the body that has a specific function or effect on other cells or body processes.

Hyperparathyroidism A bone-thinning medical condition characterized by too-low levels of calcium in the blood.

Hyperthyroidism A medical condition caused by an overactive thyroid gland.

Hypothyroidism A medical condition caused by an underactive thyroid gland.

Inappetence Lack of appetite, often one of the first noticeable signs of illness in a cat.

Insulin A chemical produced by the pancreas important in regulating blood sugar levels.

Intact The sexual status of a male or female cat when it has not been neutered or spayed; also referred to as "whole."

Intravenous A method of administering fluids or medications by injecting them into a blood vein.

Kilocalorie (kcal) The unit of measure generally used to express the energy content of food, equal to 1,000 small calories and also known as a "big calorie."

Kitten A young cat before it reaches full maturity, which generally occurs between approximately six months and one year of age.

Lactase An enzyme that helps break down lactose or milk sugar.

Lactation Milk production for the nursing of kittens.

Lactose Milk sugar; an ingredient in milk to which some adult cats become intolerant; lactose intolerant cats experience bouts of diarrhea whenever they drink milk.

Lipids Dietary fats found in foods.

Menadione A synthetic form of Vitamin K.

Metabolism A set of complex chemical processes carried on within the body's cells that converts nutrients into energy and provides energy for a variety of functions vital to life.

Minerals Inorganic chemical elements or compounds important in nutrition because of their role in maintaining certain vital body functions.

Misbranded Bearing a false, misleading, or incomplete pet food label.

Neutering The surgical removal of a male cat's testicles so that he cannot reproduce.

Obesity A medical condition characterized by excess body fat.

Ovaries The female cat's reproductive organs that produce eggs.

Palatability An assessment of how appealing a food is to the taste buds.

Parasite An organism, such as a flea or a tapeworm, that carries out part or all of its life cycle on or inside a host animal, usually to the detriment of the host.

Persian A longhaired breed of cat characterized by its rounded head, flat face, and short, cobby body.

Phylloquinone A natural form of Vitamin K.

Propylene glycol A chemical preservative no longer used as a preservative in semimoist cat foods; also the main ingredient used in "safer" antifreeze brands.

Protein A complex chain of amino acids essential to tissue growth and repair and other important body processes.

Purebred Having parents and an ancestry belonging to the same breed of cat.

Pyridoxine Vitamin B6.

Queen A female cat.

Rendering The process of cooking animal tissues at high temperatures to separate the fat from the protein.

Riboflavin Vitamin B2.

Roughage Bulky food that is high in fiber, generally consumed to stimulate the movement of food through the digestive tract.

Somali A recognized breed of cat often described as a longhaired Abyssinian.

Spaying The surgical removal of a female cat's ovaries and uterus so that she cannot produce kittens.

Testicles The male cat's reproductive glands responsible for producing sperm.

Thiamine Vitamin B1.

Tocopherol Vitamin E, often used in pet foods as a preservative to prevent fat rancidity.

Tom A male cat.

Toxic Poisonous or capable of causing detrimental or lethal effects, whether chemical, bacterial, or metabolic in origin.

Vacuum packing A packaging method that extends shelf life and reduces storage volume by using a gas to displace all air in a product's package so that no air is left inside when it is sealed.

Vitamins Organic substances derived from the diet or produced within the body that are important in nutrition because of their vital role in regulating certain metabolic functions and other body processes.

Weaning A natural process, usually completed by the age of 6 to 8 weeks, during which kittens learn to eat solid food and become less dependent on their mother's milk.

Cat Food Manufacturers

The following list is only a partial one and is not intended to endorse or exclude any particular pet food product, brand name, or manufacturer. Most of the pet food manufacturers listed below responded to the author's request for information about their products. Those not on the list either chose not to respond, could not be reached, or their company name and address were unknown at the time the list was compiled.

Bil-Jac Foods, Inc.
Kelly Foods Corp.
Berlin, MD 21811
(800) 321-1002
(Bil-Jac)

Buckeye Feed Mills, Inc.
PO Box 505
Dalton, OH 44618
(800) 898-2487
(Buckeye Feline Supreme, Buckeye Seafood Platter)

Diamond Pet Foods
Professional Pet Foods
Meta, MO 65058
(800) 442-0402, (800) 342-4808
(Diamond, Professional)

Friskies PetCare Company, Inc.
Consumer Services
800 North Brand Blvd.
Glendale, CA 91203-1244
(818) 549-6818
(Friskies, Fancy Feast, Alpo)

Fromm Family Foods
PO Box 365
Mequon, WI 53092
(800) 325-6331
(Fromm Family Nutritionals)

Heinz Pet Products
One Riverfront Place
Newport, KY 41071
(800) 252-7022
(9-Lives, Amoré)

Hill's Pet Products, Inc.
PO Box 148
Topeka, KS 66601
(800) 255-0449, (800) 445-5777
(Science Diet, Prescription Diet)

Iams Company
7250 Poe Avenue
Dayton, OH 45414-5801
(800) 525-4267, (513) 898-7387
(Iams, Eukanuba)

Kal Kan Foods
(WALTHAM U.S.A., Inc.)
3250 E. 44th Street
PO Box 58853
Vernon, CA 90058-0853
(800) 525-5273, (213) 587-2727
(Kal Kan, Whiskas, Sheba, Waltham
  Veterinary Diets)

Midwestern Pet Foods, Inc.
Evansville, IN 47711
(800) 474-4163, ext. 450
(PRO PAC Cat)

Natural Life Pet Products
PO Box 943
Frontenac, KS 66763-0943
(800) 367-2391, (316) 231-7711
(Kitten Formula, Feline Adult For-
  mula, Lamaderm Feline Formula)

Natura Pet Products
PO Box 271
Santa Clara, CA 95052
(408) 261-0770
(Innova Feline, Matrix)

Nature's Recipe Pet Foods
341 Bonnie Circle
Corona, CA 91720-2895
(800) 843-4008, (909) 278-4280
(Original Nature's Recipe, Optimum)

Nutro Products, Inc.
445 Wilson Way
City of Industry, CA 91744
(800) 833-5330
(MAX Cat, Natural Choice)

PetGuard, Inc.
PO Box 728
Orange Park, FL 32067-0728
(800) 874-3221, (800) 331-7527,
(904) 264-8500
(PetGuard Premium)

Pet Products Plus, Inc.
1600 Heritage Landing, Suite 112
St. Charles, MO 63303
(800) 592-6687
(Excel, Sensible Choice)

Pet Specialties, Inc.
24843 Del Prado #326
Dana Point, CA 92629
(800) 489-2770
(ANF, Tamiami)

Ralston Purina Company
Checkerboard Square
St. Louis, MO 63164-0001
(800) 778-7462
(Purina Cat Chow brands, Purina
  Kitten Chow, Meow Mix, Alley
  Cat, O.N.E. Premium, CNM Vet-
  erinary Diets, Pro Plan)

Vet's Choice
An affiliate of VCA
3420 Ocean Park Boulevard,
Ste. 1000
Santa Monica, CA 90405
(800) 494-PETS, (310) 392-0266
(Select Balance, Select Care)

Useful Addresses and Literature

Organizations

American Humane Society
PO Box 1266
Denver, CO 80201
(303) 695-0811

American Society for the Prevention
of Cruelty to Animals (ASPCA)
424 East 92nd Street
New York, NY 10128
(212) 876-7700

Association of American Feed
Control Officials, Inc. (AAFCO)
c/o Georgia Department of
Agriculture
Agriculture Building, Capitol Square
Atlanta, GA 30334

Cornell Feline Health Center
Cornell University College of
Veterinary Medicine
Ithaca, NY 14853
(607) 253-3414

The Delta Society
PO Box 1080
Renton, WA 98057
(206) 226-7357

Food and Drug Administration's
Center for Veterinary Medicine
(FDA-CVM)
7500 Standish Place
Rockville, MD 20855

The Humane Society of the United
States (HSUS)
2100 L Street, NW
Washington, DC 20037
(202) 452-1100

Morris Animal Foundation
45 Inverness Drive, East
Englewood, CO 80112-5480
(800) 243-2345

National Animal Poison Control
Center
University of Illinois College of
Veterinary Medicine
2001 South Lincoln Avenue
Urbana, IL 61801
(800) 548-2423
(900) 680-0000
*Note: Fee charged for crisis
management*

National Research Council (NRC)
2101 Constitution Avenue, NW
Washington, DC 20418
(202) 334-2000

Pet Food Institute
1200 19th Street, NW, Suite 300
Washington, DC 20036
(202) 857-1120

WALTHAM Centre for Pet Nutrition
Waltham-on-the-Wolds
Melton Mowbray
Leicestershire, England
http://www.waltham.com

Cat Publications
CATS Magazine
Subscriptions:
PO Box 420240
Palm Coast, FL 32142-0240
(904) 445-2818
Editorial offices:
PO Box 290037
Port Orange, FL 32129-0037
(904) 788-2770

Cat Fancy
Subscriptions:
PO Box 52864
Boulder, CO 80322-2864
(303) 666-8504
Editorial offices:
PO Box 6050
Mission Viejo, CA 92690
(714) 855-8822

Cat Fancier's Almanac
Cat Fanciers' Association
1805 Atlantic Avenue
PO Box 1005
Manasquan, NJ 08736-0805
(908) 528-9797

Catnip (newsletter)
Tufts University School of
    Veterinary Medicine
Subscriptions:
PO Box 420014
Palm Coast, FL 32142-0014
(800) 829-0926
Editorial offices:
300 Atlantic Street, 10th Floor
Stamford, CT 06901
(203) 353-6650

CatWatch (newsletter)
Cornell University College of
    Veterinary Medicine
Subscriptions:
PO Box 420235
Palm Coast, FL 32142-0235
(800) 829-8893
Editorial offices:
Torstar Publications, Inc.
99 Hawley Lane
Stratford, CT 06497

CATsumer Report
PO Box 10069
Austin, TX 78766-1069
(800) 968-1738

Books for Further Reading

Association of American Feed Control Officials, Inc. (AAFCO) *Official Publication* (published annually). For order form or purchasing information, write: AAFCO, c/o Georgia Department of Agriculture, Agriculture Building, Capitol Square, Atlanta, GA 30334.

Behrend, Katrin and Wegler, Monika. *The Complete Book of Cat Care.* Hauppauge, NY: Barron's Educational Series, Inc., 1991.

Burger, I. H., ed. *The Waltham Book of Companion Animal Nutrition.* New York: Pergamon Press, 1995.

Carlson, Delbert G., D.V.M., and Giffin, James M., M.D. *Cat Owner's Veterinary Handbook.* New York: Howell Book House, 1983.

Robinson, I., ed. *The Waltham Book of Human-Animal Interaction: Benefits and Responsibilities of Pet Ownership.* Pergamon Press, 1995.

Siegal, Mordecai and Cornell University. *The Cornell Book of Cats.* New York: Villard Books, 1989.

Subcommittee on Cat Nutrition, National Research Council. *Nutrient Requirements of Cats, Revised Edition, 1986.* For information, write: National Academy Press, 2101 Constitution Avenue, NW, Washington, DC 20418.

Taylor, David. *The Ultimate Cat Book.* New York: Simon and Schuster, 1989.

Taylor, David. *You & Your Cat: A Complete Guide to the Health, Care & Behavior of Cats.* New York: Alfred A. Knopf, 1986.

Thorne, C., ed. *The Waltham Book of Dog and Cat Behaviour.* New York: Pergamon Press, 1992.

Whiteley, H. Ellen, D.V.M. *Understanding and Training Your Cat or Kitten.* New York: Crown Trade Paperbacks, 1994.

Wills, Josephine M. and Simpson, Kenneth W., eds. *The Waltham Book of Clinical Nutrition of the Dog & Cat.* New York: Pergamon Press, 1994.

Wright, Michael and Walters, Sally, eds. *The Book of the Cat.* New York: Summit Books, 1980.

Index

154